CAREER QUEST

MARY ROSE REMINGTON

CAREER QUEST

A Practical and Spiritual Guide
to Finding Your Life's Passion

Mary Rose Remington

 HEARTWOOD PUBLISHING, St. Paul, Minnesota

 HEARTWOOD PUBLISHING, St. Paul, MN

Copyright © 2003 by Mary Rose Remington

Book design, cover art and illustrations by Kathleen Hanson

Printed in the United States of America

Library of Congress Control Number: 2003114693

ISBN 0-9746548-0-9

10   9   8   7   6   5   4   3   2   1

First Edition

Dedication

To my husband Greg… who already knows
the many reasons why.

And to my daughter Laura and sons Kevin and
Tyler. Thanks for the gift of space, solitude and
support when I needed it most –
and for your love.

TABLE OF CONTENTS

Acknowledgements

To the Creator of all that is good, I pray this book is a worthy offering in thanksgiving for a life rich with blessings.

Writing is a solitary act, yet this book is the fruit of many who collaborated. Career Quest had a long gestational period, nurtured along by great friends and loving family members who provided the encouragement I needed to counteract multiple rejections and setbacks.

I am grateful to my clients and students, for teaching me that each journey is unique, yet similar. It has been both an honor and privilege to work with and learn from them.

My gratitude runs deep for the The Loft Literary Center in Minneapolis. This book would not have happened without the monastic studios and their artist-in-residency grant; lifesavers tossed to me when I was drowning. And heartfelt appreciation to Robert Hedin, director of the Anderson Center for the Arts, for the spiritually serene environment to write in.

When the book neared completion, three competent women stepped in to tackle the hard work. I'm eternally endebted to Kathleen Hanson for formatting and cover design, my editor Cindy Rogers for making me look good, and Lisa Daily, publicist extraordinaire.

Many thanks to Jeremy Taylor, for permission to publish his hints on dreams and to Howard Gardner for use of his eight types of intelligence.

PART 1

Passionate Work™

CLAIM YOUR BIRTHRIGHT

CHAPTER 1

Core Beliefs

"I love my job!" Years ago when I heard people say this I thought they were lying — or at least exaggerating. Stuck in a confining corporate job, I couldn't even say I liked let alone loved my job. I settled for less, because at the time I couldn't imagine anything better.

Admittedly not everything about my old job was horrible. It was close to home, provided a steady (although puny) paycheck and flexible hours, which was important with three small kids. As my work environment got progressively worse, I rationalized my decision to stay by telling myself:

"In order to have the flexibility to take care of my family, I must put up with this negative job."

"A great deal depends upon the thought patterns we choose and on the persistence with which we affirm them."

Pierro Ferrucci

This statement was my core belief; a belief that was both limiting and untrue. My belief kept me stuck in a job far too small for my spirit. Eventually the stress at work forced me to quit and start my own company. Today as a freelance writer and author, career counselor and life coach, instructor and public speaker I can honestly say, "I love my job!" Now I understand that the world is abundant and can meet all my needs. My core belief has changed. It is possible to have the flexibility I need to care for my family while doing work I love!

I believe everyone is entitled to passionate work. Trust that you will be rewarded on your career quest and find work you love, the work you came to earth to do. Passionate work is your birthright, and it all begins with your core beliefs.

> *"Life is a promise. Fulfill it."*
>
> Mother Teresa

Importance of Core Beliefs

Core beliefs are a person's innermost convictions about how life works. It is our mental acceptance of truth or reality. Core beliefs are powerful in that they drive our thoughts, behaviors and expectations. What we get out of life depends upon what we expect to get. Core beliefs are the foundation upon which we launch our personal and professional lives. Core beliefs can be

- Positive or Negative
- Abundant or Limiting
- Conscious or Unconscious
- Helpful or Harmful
- Accurate or False

Core beliefs can often be limiting or false, just like mine were. In your quest for passionate work it will be important for you to uncover, examine and possibly revise your core beliefs.

Where Core Beliefs Come From

Society, friends and family member influence our core beliefs. Your family of origin — especially your parents — played a crucial role in shaping your core beliefs. For better or worse, your parents guided your perception about how the world works and what you are entitled to.

Most parents fall under one of three categories: absent, negative or positive. Which category best describes your parents?

Absent or Apathetic

These parents showed little or no interest in their child. They may have been physically absent due to work commitments or emotionally unavailable due to alcohol, drugs or mental/physical illness. If you had parents like this, you learned to look elsewhere for guidance or you simply struggled on your own.

If you had absent parents your core beliefs may be:

- "I'm not worthy of people's time or energy."
- "I have to find my own way in life."
- "I'm not entitled to help."

However, just the opposite is true.
You *are* worthy of people's time and energy.
You *do not* have to find your way alone in life. You *are* entitled to help and *it is* fine to ask for it.

Negative

Your parents fit this category if their advice always began with "don't."

- "Don't get your hopes up."
- "Don't count your chickens before they're hatched."
- "Don't come crying to me when you fall flat on your face."

If you had negative parents your core beliefs may include:

- "If I don't expect much out of life, I won't be disappointed."
- "If I don't take risks, I'll never fail."
- "Things never work out, so I shouldn't even try."

Unfortunately, if you don't expect much out of life, you won't get much. And in order to succeed, you must take risks.

Positive

Perhaps your parents worked hard to nurture you. Positive parents help their children recognize their unique talents and abilities while spreading an optimistic, can-do attitude. If you had parents like this your core beliefs may sound like:

- "If I'm persistent, I can accomplish anything!"
- "It's ok for me to try something new and ask for help."
- "I am entitled to a good life."

Rewriting Core Beliefs

Your parents have influenced your core beliefs, but core beliefs are not caste in stone. Examine your core beliefs, and then decide if you want to keep or rewrite them. If the core beliefs you inherited about life are positive, supportive, and they work for you – great! Embrace them and pass them on to the next generation. But if you inherited negative, unsupportive beliefs that undermine your ability to get what you want from life, it's time to stop the cycle. You can rewrite your core beliefs with this four-step approach.

1. Identify and write down your negative belief.
2. Name who gave it to you.
3. Mentally send it back to them (even if they are no longer alive).
4. Rewrite a positive version of the negative belief.

The beauty of rewriting core beliefs is this: You don't even have to believe it at first. You simply state how you want things to work. By stating positive beliefs over and over again you actually begin to manifest what you want and how you want things to turn out.

> *"It's never too late – in fiction or in life – to revise."*
>
> Nancy Thayer

Example

1. Write out negative core belief

   "Once you have a family, you have to give up doing what you love in order to support them."

2. Name the origin: *from Dad.*

3. Give it back: *"Dad, this belief is yours, not mine; so I'm sending it back to you. I choose not to believe it because it doesn't work for me."*

4. Revised, positive belief: *"It is possible to support my family doing what I love."*

Now try one of your own.

1. *Identify a negative core belief you'd like to revise.*

   _____

   _____

   _____

   _____

2. *Who gave it to you? (origin)*

   _____

3. *This belief is not mine. It belongs to*

   _____

   I respectfully send it back. It doesn't work for me and I don't believe it.

4. *My revised, positive core belief is*

   _____

   _____

   _____

   _____

   _____

Undoubtedly, we become what we envisage.

Claude M. Bristol

Pardon Me. Your Core Belief is Showing.

When I speak to groups about passionate work, inevitably someone from the audience comes up afterward and they explain – with great conviction – why they can't *possibly* search for work they love. People's core beliefs surface when they share their comments. I've listed a few of my favorites below. After their comment, I list their probable core belief, respond to their comment and give a revised, positive core belief.

COMMENT 1

"I hate my job, but I've been there twenty years. I have seniority, fairly decent income plus three weeks of vacation every year. Why should I risk all that?"

Core Belief

Security is everything. My personal satisfaction doesn't count for anything.

My Response

Unfortunately in today's work-world, seniority is no longer a guarantee of employment. Besides, is it worth being unhappy for 49 weeks out of the year just to have three weeks off?

Revised, Positive Core Belief

The world is abundant and can provide me with a job that is personally satisfying, pays well and gives me as much time off as I want.

COMMENT 2

"There are a lot of cruddy jobs out there. Somebody has to do them!"

Core Belief

There are many bad jobs in the world and I can't expect anything more.

My Response

If you lived next door to a single person you despised, would you feel obligated to marry this person? Then why do you feel obligated to take a cruddy job you don't like?"

Revised, Positive Core Belief

The world has many wonderful jobs to offer. I'm entitled to work I love.

COMMENT 3

"I despise my job, but I'm only seven years away from retirement. I'm just going to try and hang in there."

Core Belief

Work is something to be endured.

My Response

I hate to imagine what kind of physical and mental condition you'll be in after seven more years at a job you despise. What are the odds that you'll be well enough (or even around) to enjoy your retirement?

Revised, Positive Core Belief

Every day is precious. I'm entitled to spend my remaining workdays doing something I love.

COMMENT 4

"Work is supposed to be difficult. That's why they call it work!"

Core Belief

Work is hard. It's ridiculous to expect anything better.

My Response

Question: Where did this belief that "work is supposed to be difficult" come from? Is it yours

> "*While it's true you can't change the effect past influences had on you once, you can change the effect they have on you now.*"
>
> *Gary McKay*

or did someone give this belief to you?

Does it work for you?

Positive Core Belief

Work can be fun, easy and satisfying.

Now it's your turn

Do you have an old, negative core belief about work that you'd like to revise?

List it here.

_____

_____

_____

_____

_____

_____

Rewrite your negative core belief into a positive, abundant statement. This is your new and improved positive core belief.

_____

_____

_____

_____

_____

_____

_____

Word Power

When we look at the definition our society gives to work, it's easy to see why people have such negative expectations about employment. Here's the definition as stated in the American Heritage Dictionary: "Physical or mental effort or activity directed towards the production or accomplishment of something – to toil, labor. Employment; a job...a trade, craft, business or profession. Not terribly exciting.

And just look at the dreary picture the following synonyms paint about work. Drudgery, effort, exertion, grind, plod, slavery, strain, struggle, sweat, toil, labor, chore and travail (which means to work involving great effort pain and suffering).

I doubt our Creator intended for us to spend 60% of our lives at jobs that cause us great pain and suffering!

When searching for words that describe work in a positive way, I find only two.

1. Livelihood:
   - Means of support; subsistence
   - Course of life, sustenance, life course

2. Vocation:
   - A regular occupation or profession; especially one for which one is especially suited or qualified.
   - An urge or predisposition to undertake a certain kind of work, especially a religious career
   - A calling.

The word vocation is derived from the Latin word "vocation," meaning "to call." Vocation is often used in connection with people joining religious orders, who frequently state they felt called to join,

> *It's a funny thing about life; if you refuse to accept anything but the best, you very often get it."*
>
> Somerset Maugham

as if the religious life chose them. You might not feel called to join a religious order, but you do have a specific calling awaiting you. The question is, will you answer the call?

CHAPTER 2

Wake-Up Calls

Learning Lessons and Giving Back

I believe we agree on a soul level to come to earth, a place that compared to heaven is tremendously difficult and painful. But we choose to incarnate for three reasons: to learn specific lessons, to develop as souls and to give something back. Before we are even born our Soul or Higher Self, with assistance from the Divine, chooses our parents, siblings, lovers, co-workers and other significant people we'll live out our life with. We even orchestrate ahead of time life events that will provide learning opportunities for the lessons we need to master.

Besides coming here to learn lessons, we also come to give something back. This giving back to humanity involves our mission or higher purpose, which will be covered in Chapter 3. Free will allows us to accept or reject our mission. However, when we reject the work we contracted to do, the Creator attempts to get us back on track with what I call "God's little nudges." At first the incidents start out mild, but if we ignore them, they get stronger and more painful in order to get our attention.

Reverend Tom Hyder from Minneapolis explains, "In my work as a spiritual healer, it's been my experience that Spirit will often orchestrate an

> *"For our own good, each of us needs to learn what our mission is, because the details of how we live our lives accumulate to create health or illness. The further we stray from our mission in life, the more frustrated we will become and the more out of sync our energy will be."*
>
> *Caroline Myss*

illness or accident when it is time for our wake-up call." Hyder explains that Spirit is our core essence: It is our innate wisdom or consciousness that connects us to our divine essence, our Soul. He says, "Spirit is the spark of life within us that as we begin to look inside and listen will lead us to healing, to wholeness, to holiness."

He goes on to explain about wake up calls. "As we get knocked out of our daily pattern and begin to search for reasons, it is the very search that will begin us on our path of remembering we are truly spiritual beings in physical form." It is our Spirit that helps us see when we are not living the life we should be.

Caroline Myss, author of *Sacred Contracts* says it this way. "We can either take the path of wisdom or woe." In other words, heed the message and wisdom of the wake-up calls, or they'll eventually get worse, leading to the path of woe.

Numerous Rounds of Wake-Up Calls

It took several rounds of wake-up calls for me to finally get the message that I needed to leave my corporate job. Over the course of three years, minor problems at work developed into major ones. I worked for toxic managers and the building I worked in had constant environmental problems that caused headaches, fatigue and allergies for many of us. While pregnant with my third child, I even suffered pre-term labor from all the stress. But fear, lack of faith and negative core beliefs kept me stuck, until I had three near-miss-car-accidents in one week. Intuitively I just knew that these near misses were meant to shake me up enough to quit my job. Although it was frightening at the time, leaving was the right decision. Once I quit my job, the wake-up calls ceased. I've never, ever looked back.

An Analogy

Imagine a mother trapped in a burning building with her daughter. The firefighters below have nets in place and are yelling, "Jump! We'll catch you!" The mother directs her child towards the window and explains that they both must jump or they'll die. She nudges her daughter onto the window ledge, reassures her that the fire fighters will catch her and encourages her to jump. But her daughter is still too afraid to leap. As the flames creep near and time runs out, the mother eventually grabs her daughter and pushes her out the window to the safety of the nets below.

I believe the Creator acts the same way when we are in work or life situations that aren't good for us. First we are given whispering insights, and given the chance to "leap" on our own. But if we don't heed the signs, the wake-up calls get louder and more severe, to the point we cannot ignore them. If we don't jump on our own, the Creator finds ways to push us out – for our own good.

> *"The first wealth is health."*
>
> *Ralph Waldo Emerson*

Kenny Loggins, singer and songwriter wrote, "Pain is intended to be a mover, not a permanent place of residence." Trust that the painful situation you are experiencing has been designed by the Creator and your Higher Self to prod you on to something better.

Health Matters

Clients describe to me how their energy drains the closer they get to work. Unfortunately, that energy drain can develop into a physical illness. Our bodies "act up" to alert us when something is out of sync in our lives.

Barbara Ann Brennan, healer and author of *Hands of Light* and *Light Emerging* says, "It is essential that we deal with the deeper meaning of our illnesses. We need to ask, what does this illness mean to me? What can I learn from this illness? An illness usually means that we are ignoring something very important and we need to get at the source in order to return to complete health." According to Brennan, "to deal with the source usually requires a life change that ultimately leads to a personal life more connected to the core of one's being. It leads us to that deeper part of ourselves that is sometimes called the high self or the spark of divinity."

When our bodies present us with ailments or illness as a wake up call, we have two choices. We can either:

1. Honor the symptoms, listen to what our body is telling us and take corrective action.

2. Or ignore the physical symptoms and wait for the illness or injury to get worse. And if the illness has been sent as a wake-up call, it will get progressively worse until we heed the message.

True Stories

Most of my clients striving to make career changes have at least one physical ailment coinciding with their work situation. One young woman said, "I break out in hives every time I even think about work! It's as if I'm allergic to my job."

Another middle-aged woman admitted, "I'm actually looking forward to having cancer surgery. At least it will give me a break from work!"

One man labored for decades at a stressful job, but couldn't muster up the courage to quit – until he was diagnosed with chronic fatigue syndrome. He admits it was a difficult way out.

I worked with a woman who suffered not one, but two debilitating strokes before she finally left her life-threatening job.

Personal Health Pulse

My goal is to get people to face reality and deal with their health issues before they get worse. Here are some typical health problems that people in negative, stressful work situations experience. Circle all that you've experienced in the last three years.

Physical health issues

- Fatigue
- Allergies/Asthma
- Skin irritations/rashes/hives
- Chronic colds/flu
- Digestive problems (ulcers, stomachaches)
- Headaches
- Heart trouble (high blood pressure, angina, palpitations, heart attacks)
- Insomnia or sleeping too much
- Back pain
- Menstrual difficulties
- Laryngitis
- Broken bones, sprains
- Carpal tunnel syndrome
- Thyroid disorders

Are you currently experiencing any other health problems? Describe them below.

_____

_____

Have they gotten better or worse in the last three months?

_____

Do you believe there is an underlying message to your illness?

_____

What is your illness trying to tell you?

_____

_____

_____

_____

Wake-up Calls Come In Many Forms

In addition to health problems, there are a variety of negative life events that can also serve as wake-up calls. Circle all that you've experienced in the past two or three years.

- Layoff/work force reduced
- Termination
- Reporting to an awful manager
- Intense, unresolved problems with co-workers
- Divorce or separation
- Mental health issues
  - Depression
  - Anxiety
  - Panic attacks
- Car accidents
- Death of a loved one
- Financial difficulties, bankruptcy
- Home or office hit by fire, flood, tornado or other natural disasters

What other negative life events have you experienced in the last three years? List them below.

_____

_____

_____

_____

_____

Do they seem to be getting more frequent?

_____

_____

_____

What do you think the underlying message is?

_____

_____

_____

God uses these negative wake-up calls for our highest good, to get us moving towards our destiny. No doubt you feel your life is chaotic and painful. But let's face it: if you were feeling comfortable you wouldn't budge, would you?

"There is nothing the body suffers which the soul may not profit from."

George Meredith

As you stand at the fork in your career crossroad, you have two choices.

1. You can continue on the same path, do what you've always done, stay in the same job or look for another one just like it. This choice will bring you more of the same: more health

problems, more crises and more wake up calls.

2. Or you can forge a new career path on the road that is right for you.

The Chinese have two symbols for crisis: one is danger; the other is opportunity. Consider this crises your opportunity to seek passionate work: the work you came to do. Working everyday at a job you despise will affect your mental and physical health and taint the quality of your life. Eleanor Roosevelt said, "We are each responsible for the decisions we make." Take responsibility for your choices, your life, your health and happiness. As you move forward on your career quest, trust yourself to start making better decisions.

CHAPTER 3

Unlocking Your Higher Purpose

- **Reason for living**
- **Life work**
- **Sacred contract**
- **Calling**
- **Mission in life**

These are all different ways to describe higher purpose, or the work we came to earth to do. Our higher purpose is a built-in reason for being, and once unlocked provides a compelling reason to get up each morning. Everyone has a higher purpose, which starts with an inherent desire to make a contribution to the world. We all want our life to count for something. Those who seem happiest and most satisfied have found something significant to dedicate their life, energy and talents toward.

Dick Leider, author of *The Power of Purpose* writes, "Purpose is the conscious choice of how to make a positive contribution to our world. When we work on purpose we bring together the needs of the world with our special talents in a vocation or calling. To find purpose, we need to discover our talents and what moves us – our passions." Richard Bolles, author of the best-selling book on

> *"We each have been put here on earth to fulfill a sacred contract that enhances our spiritual growth, while contributing to the evolution of the entire global soul."*
>
> Caroline Myss, author of
> Sacred Contracts

careers, *What Color Is Your Parachute* describes it this way: "The gifts of each of us, plus the value of serving others provide our mission in life."

Purpose Involves Talents, Passion and Service

Your higher purpose will involve a combination of your unique talents, passion for the work and service to humanity, covered in Chapters 4-6. Have faith. Trust that you have the ability, inclination and passion for the work you came to do. Rumi said it well, "Everyone has been made for some particular work and the desire for that work has been put in his [her] heart."

How Do I Find My Higher Purpose?

I teach a class to help adults make career changes. One woman in her forties sheepishly confessed to me after class, "I was hoping we could just fill out a questionnaire and a computer would spit out our higher purpose for us."

It isn't that simple. There are no short cuts, no easy answers and no computer program to spit out the answer. But know this: you do have a higher purpose and you carry the answer within.

In the movie *Pay It Forward*, a middle-school teacher challenges his seventh grade class with this assignment: "Think of an idea to change our world and put it into action." The teacher asks students to consider this: "What if you take what you don't like about the world, and flip it right on its ass. The realm of possibility exists in each of you. Surprise us."

In the movie, each child comes up with a different way to change the world. The lead character designs a simple strategy called "pay it forward." He does favors for three people and asks them to

> *"The journey of spiritual growth requires courage and initiative and independence of thought and action."*
>
> M. Scott Peck

pay it forward by doing a favor for three additional people. His plan has profound, life-saving effects that reach across the country.

To find your higher purpose, that teacher's assignment is what you must do. Think of an idea to change the world and put it into action. Find what you don't like about the world and strive to make it better. Find a need. Then fill it.

Begin At The End

One way to search for your higher purpose is to fast-forward to the end of your life. Everyone wants his or her life to count. No one wants to be on their deathbed and say, "Oh, darn, I forgot to make a difference." So begin the quest for your higher purpose by contemplating these four questions:

1. *When I die, what do I want people to say about me?*

_____

_____

_____

2. *What legacy do I want to leave behind, both personally and professionally?*

_____

_____

_____

3. *How will the world be better off because I was here?*

_____

_____

_____

_____

4. *What do I want people to say I valued, stood*
    for and accomplished with my life?

_____

_____

_____

_____

Think of your life today as you answer these questions:

When you read the newspapers or watch the news,
what stories pull on your heartstrings the hardest?

_____

_____

_____

_____

"Each of us must
make his own path
through life. There are
no self-help manuals,
no formulas, no easy
answers."

M. Scott Peck

What situations can you hardly stand to hear about?

_____

_____

_____

What societal injustices anger you to the point of
action?

_____

_____

_____

_____

To which charities do you already donate money and
time?

_____

_____

_____

If you won the lottery, which causes would you dedicate time, money and energy?

_____

_____

_____

_____

What is the Creator calling you to do more of? Less of?

_____

_____

_____

_____

What is your deepest heart's desire for humanity?

_____

_____

_____

_____

Personal and Professional Missions

Most people have one primary, higher purpose. How and where it's worked out depends upon their generation and life circumstances. For example, my mother-in-law, who is in her seventies, spent her life raising thirteen children, helped nurture over thirty grandchildren, volunteered in countless community efforts and dedicated more than a year of her life to taking care of her dying sister. Had she been born one generation later, I suspect she might have raised a slightly smaller family and had a nursing or social work career. Yet the fact that she didn't get paid for her mission does not detract from the importance of it. In many ways, it adds to it.

> *"The place God calls you to, is the place where your deep gladness and the world's deep hunger meet."*
>
> *Frederick Buechner*

Not everyone will be called to a higher purpose involving high and mighty acts. Parenting is a good example of a higher purpose that involves simple, often mundane tasks. Yet what could be greater than bringing a child into the world and raising him or her in a loving, supportive, dedicated manner?

It isn't important whether you fulfill your higher purpose as a paid professional, a private citizen or as a volunteer. What matters is that you do it.

Honor Your Energy

Finding your higher purpose and life work is similar to falling in love. Hardly anyone marries the first person they date. Likewise, you probably won't find your higher purpose at your first job. But feel free to look around. Try different careers. Take up a new hobby. Explore intriguing activities. Volunteer. Keep searching, studying and exploring while paying attention to your energy in all your endeavors.

Simply put, if it feels good, rewarding, satisfying and energizing, it's a yes. If it feels bad, unrewarding, unsatisfying and draining, then it's a no. Think about people you know who are clear about their purpose in life. They are energized and passionate about what they're doing, and their lives radiate with a sense of devotion and meaning. That's what you are seeking: a career where your actions and energies are aligned with activities that are purposeful, meaningful and valuable.

Mitch Album, author of *Tuesdays with Morrie*, captures the wisdom of life in this quote from his dying professor Morrie Schultz: "So many people walk around with a meaningless life. They seem half asleep, even when they're busy doing things they think are important. This is because they are chasing the wrong things. The way you get meaning into your life is to devote yourself to loving others, devote yourself to the community around you and devote yourself to creating something that gives you purpose and meaning."

Inspirational Drip

Expect inspiration to come, but understand that the Divine works more like a dripping faucet than like Niagra Falls. Inspiration will come, drip...drip...drip...one insight at a time. Have patience, be persistent and mindful of your energy. Spend time in solitude, meditation or prayer and believe the answer to your higher purpose awaits discovery within you.

Work involving your higher purpose has a wonderful feel to it. Watch for these important clues:

- You'll feel good about yourself and the service you are providing.

- All – not just some – of your unique talents and creativity will be used.

- The tasks will challenge and stretch you in a healthy way.

- Work will be fun, sacred and soulful and won't feel like work.

- If you become independently wealthy, you'll still be compelled to participate in this endeavor.

- Work will be meaningful and help you evolve personally.

- People will comment on how good you look. They'll say things like "Have you lost weight? You look great!"

- The boundaries between work, life and play will blur.

ъ▪ You'll be extremely energized, often to the point of needing less sleep, forgetting to eat, etc.

ъ▪ You'll lose all track of time.

RECOMMENDED READING

- *The Power of Purpose- Creating Meaning in Your Life and Work*   by Richard J. Leider

PART 2

Divine Formula

TALENTS + PASSIONS + SERVICE

CHAPTER 4

Unique Talents

Born and Blessed

Trust the Divine Creator. You were born and blessed with the inherent talent necessary to complete your mission. You have what you need within you. By all means, develop your talent with education and training, but understand this: your inherent abilities are within you, even before you show up in any classroom.

My son Kevin demonstrated this on his first day of school. Many of the kindergarten students were distressed at being separated from their parents. Since Kevin had attended pre-school and had already worked through his separation anxiety, he went around the room and "counseled" his crying schoolmates. "There, there, I know it's hard, but your mom will be back later. Why don't we put this puzzle together." At the tender age of 5, my son was already demonstrating his counseling skills.

Discernment

Although you have what you need, you may not realize all that you have. On the journey to passionate work, you will be called to discern your gifts. Discernment is the process of discovering, acknowledging and accepting your aptitudes and talents; things you are naturally good at.

"Purpose and calling seem at first glance grand words, best reserved for a gifted few. But we all possess an ability to do the work we were made for."

Richard Leider, author of The Power of Purpose.

41

Drop the Modesty

Sadly, most people have been socialized to downplay or negate their abilities. Adults scold their children with words like, ""Don't brag!" "Quite being so cocky." "Modesty is the best policy." Sound familiar?

Author Mary McCarthy details her years as an orphan in her book *Memories of a Catholic Girlhood*. Due to her parent's untimely death, her neglectful aunt and abusive uncle raised her. This horrible scene follows a school celebration where she was awarded a prize for her written essay: "When we came to our ugly house, my uncle silently rose from his chair, led me into the dark downstairs lavatory, which always smelled of shaving cream, and furiously beat me with the razor strop. "To teach me a lesson," he said, "lest I become stuck-up." Extreme? Yes. Unheard of? Tragically, no.

As an adult, you are now safe to uncover, explore and celebrate all your unique talents. Modesty and self-deprecation will only be a hindrance. Embrace your gifts. Recognize you are a splendid creation of the Divine!

My favorite quote by Marianne Williams sums it up well. "We ask ourselves – who am I to be brilliant, gorgeous, talented, fabulous? Actually, who are you not to be? You are a child of God. Your playing small does not serve the world. There is nothing enlightened about shrinking so that other people won't feel insecure around you. We are born to make manifest the glory of God that is within us."

It's time to make manifest the glory of God within you.

> *"Pride... is the direct appreciation of oneself."*
>
> *Arthur Schopenhauer*

Multiple Talents

Considering the vast and diverse needs of this world, I find it comforting to recognize the diverse talents that exist among people. Howard Gardner, developmental psychologist with the Harvard Graduate School of Education wrote a book called *Multiple Intelligences,* that describes multiple capabilities or types of intelligences.

Eight Types of Smart

1. ### Logical/Mathematical/Science

   People with this type of intelligence are good with numbers and can think in a logical, linear manner. Traditionally, those who have exhibited this intelligence have been labeled "smart" by society.

2. ### Linguistics

   Writers, poets and editors are linguistically intelligent: they work well with words.

3. ### Visual/Spatial

   If you can read a map and don't get overwhelmed with "some assembly required" you have visual/spatial intelligence. This type is found in interior designers, sailors, engineers, sculptors, painters, mechanics and surgeons.

4. ### Musical Intelligence

   Those who can read music, carry a tune, keep a beat and/or play an instrument have musical intelligence.

5. ### Bodily/Kinesthetic

   Kinesthetic intelligence entails the use of the body in some capacity to solve a problem or perform a feat. Dancers, athletes, surgeons and

"We can't take any credit for our own talents. It's how we use them that counts."

Madleine L'Engle

craftspeople have bodily/kinesthetic intelligence. People like Michael Jordan and tennis players Serena and Venus Williams are kinesthetically talented.

6. **Interpersonal**

    This is the ability to understand other people — what motivates them, how they think, how to work cooperatively together. Successful salespeople, politicians, religious leaders, therapists, teachers and mediators tend to have high degrees of interpersonal skills.

7. **Intrapersonal**

    Simply stated, intrapersonal intelligence is the ability to know oneself. Gandhi is perhaps one of the best examples.

8. **Naturalist**

    People with this intelligence have an intuitive sense of how things fit together in the world. They know and understand what works and what doesn't work with Mother Nature.

Our Creator knew it would take a multitude of talents to make this world work, so each of us has been gifted with different abilities. Your job is to discern your unique skills and combine it with your passion in some form of service.

Questions to contemplate

1. *Which types of intelligence do people say you are blessed with?*

_____

_____

_____

_____

> *"We will discover the nature of our particular genius when we stop trying to conform to other people's models, learn to be ourselves and allow our natural channel to open."*
>
> *Shakti Gawain*

2. *What abilities do you possess, but have not used? What gets in the way of using these talents? What fears do you have about using them?*

_____

_____

_____

_____

3. *Is it possible you may have undiscovered talents and abilities?*

_____

_____

4. *What might they be?*

_____

_____

_____

_____

AVENUES FOR INFORMATION

People

Some individuals have skills that come so easily to them, they don't consider them talents. Allow friends, family, teachers, co-workers to provide positive feedback, encouragement and validation about your gifts. Listen to and graciously accept their compliments.

Experiences

No matter how old you are, don't assume you have discovered all your talents. Like many writers, I didn't recognize my talent until my mid-thirties. The book *Life Is So Good* depicts the life and times of George Dawson, grandson of an African American slave, who enrolled in a literary class at the age of 98 and learns to read for the first time in his life. By his example and enthusiasm, he inspires people in his community to take advantage of reading and educational programs, proving it's never too late to learn something new.

Heed Inclinations

Now is the time to follow your inklings. Have you always wanted to paint? Get some supplies, take a class if you like, and start painting. Fancy yourself as a writer? Who's stopping you? Start writing! Wonder if you'd be any good at landscaping? Experiment with your own yard or offer to help a friend in the landscaping business.

As you begin to explore, lower your expectations. Don't worry about doing anything perfectly – or even well — at first. Simply allow yourself to have a go at it.

You are the only person who can use your God-given abilities. The choice is yours: work on discovering your gifts or go to your grave with your talents untapped.

> *"Most people go to their graves with their music still inside them."*
>
> Oliver Wendel Homes

Journal Questions

1. *What courses did you excel in at school with little or no effort?*

_____

_____

_____

_____

_____

_____

2. *When you go to the bookstore, which sections do you naturally gravitate to?*

_____

_____

_____

_____

3. *What do people frequently ask you to help them with?*

_____

_____

_____

_____

4. *How would friends fill in the blank? "You're a natural at …"*

_____

_____

5. *Or "You'd make such a good…"*

_____

_____

RECOMMENDED READING

- *The Artist's Way* by Julia Cameron
- *Multiple Intelligences* by Howard Gardner

CHAPTER 5

Follow Your Passion

The first element of passionate work is unique talents and the second piece is love for your work. By all accounts, not many Americans have it. According to a current Wall Street Journal study, 50% of working adults said if they had a chance to choose over again, they would pick a different career. In a recent study by a New York based conference board, Americans were asked if they were satisfied with their jobs. Nationwide, only 51% said yes, compared with 59% in 1995. Conduct your own informal poll. Ask friends and family, "Do you love your job?" Chances are you'll wind up with an abundance of no's.

> "Always leave enough time in your life to do something that makes you happy, satisfied, even joyous. That has more of an effect on economic well being than any other single factor. "
>
> Paul Hawken

Energy As a Guiding Force

Honor your energy on your career quest. On the path to your purpose, pay attention to how you feel when involved in specific activities or projects. Let your personal energy serve as a compass to keep you on course. The word enthusiasm is derived from a Greek word meaning to be inspired/possessed by a god. Trust your enthusiasm as a divine sign that you are on the right path.

Take the Lottery Test

Fantasy time: If you won the lottery tomorrow and didn't have to work another day, to what activities and organizations would you dedicate your time,

> *"Only the heart knows how to find what is precious."*
>
> Fyodor Dostoyevsky

talent, energy and money?

My friend and her husband actually won 22.2 million in the Minnesota Powerball Lottery. Once the reality set in, my friend quit her job as a child rights attorney. Since she was clear about her passion and mission in life, she was not content to sit idly by. She soon began volunteering (and continues to work) at places that help children, such as crisis nurseries.

Those who work in the creative arts know what it means to be passionate about work. Artists, musicians, dancers, writers, painters, sculptors, photographers describe their work differently than most people in other professions. Many artists describe a negative, visceral reaction when separated from their craft:

Megan Flood, a professional dancer from St. Paul, MN said, "If I can't dance I feel trapped in my body." Her partner, Dean MacGraw, a musician stated, "Playing music is almost like an addiction – but without the side affects you get with drugs. It's like a "hit" of energy – a way of feeding yourself instead of killing yourself."

> *'Nothing you love should ever be left sitting on the shelf. You have a right to everything you love."*
>
> Morrie Schultz

Dave Johnson, a poet from New York equates the act of writing to a sexual charge. "It just feels biological to me, like a creative endorphin release."

Corine Duchesne, a painter from Canada summed it up definitively. "Once I started painting I was completely changed. It's almost like something picked painting for me. I don't have a choice, really. I can't give it up."

Passion = Success

Think about people you know who are extremely successful. Odds are they love their work. There is a logical and intuitive connection to passion and success. A Dutch psychologist studied what separated chess masters from chess grand masters. Each group was subjected to a battery of tests – memory, spatial reasoning and IQ. There were no differences between the chess masters and the grand masters, except one: the grand masters simply loved chess more. Passion, it seems, is the key to success.

> *"Man is not free to refuse to do the thing which gives him more pleasure than any other conceivable action."*
>
> Stendhall

Questions to contemplate:

1. *What activities do you enjoy so much you lose track of time?*

   _____

   _____

   _____

   _____

2. *Do you ever get so involved in something you forget to eat or miss sleep?*

   _____

   _____

   _____

   _____

3. *If you won the lottery, name several ways you'd fill your days.*

   _____

   _____

   _____

   _____

CHAPTER 6

Service to Others

True story. Mother Teresa was riding in a car through the streets of Calcutta with a wealthy gentleman, when suddenly the driver of their car swerved to avoid hitting a beggar in the road. Mother Teresa instructed the driver to stop. She got out, tended to the beggar's wounds, kissed him, and got back in the car. The man she was riding with said to her, "You couldn't pay me a million dollars to do what you just did." She thought for a moment and replied, "You couldn't pay me a million dollars either."

Not all of us have what Mother Teresa had. But everyone has the ability to make the world a slightly better place, by providing meaningful service to others. Everyone has a natural desire to contribute something. For many it's a developmental process: the older we get the more compelling it becomes to make a significant difference. Meaningful service to others is the third element of passionate work.

"Service is the rent we pay for room on this earth."

Shirley Chisholm

Visualize an Umbrella

Picture your Higher Purpose as the spike on top of a huge umbrella. The individual metal rods are ways in which you serve. For example, my Higher Purpose is to help people resolve career, life and spiritual issues. The specific ways I serve is through writing, teaching, speaking and individual counseling sessions.

Tapping Tragedy

- Patti Wetterling

- John Walsh

- Candy Lightner

These three people are parents with two things in common. They each suffered the tragic loss of their child and all three channeled their feelings of hatred, rage and loss into programs that help ensure the safety of other children. Instead of letting their feelings eat them alive, they applied their passion to create organizations that help others.

Patti Wetterling founded the *Jacob Wetterling Foundation* after her eleven-year old son was abducted and never found. Her mission is to educate communities about child safety and prevent child exploitation and abduction.

John Walsh, as seen on *Americas Most Wanted* and the *John Walsh* show, also became a tireless advocate for victim's rights after his son Adam was abducted and murdered in 1981.

"Concern should drive us into action, not into a depression."

Karen Horney

You may not have heard of Candy Lightner, but I'm sure you've heard of MADD, Mother's Against Drunk Drivers. Candy helped to found MADD in 1980 after her daughter Cari was killed by a drunk driver. She and the volunteers at MADD have achieved major legislative changes and have educated countless drivers about the dangers of driving under the influence.

If you've had a tragedy in your life, consider doing what these people did. Direct your energies towards resolving the very problem that led to your situation. People like Patti, John and Candy know first hand that you can either let the tragedy eat you

> *"Your greatness is measured by your service to others."*
>
> *Jesus*

making the world a better place. In the words of Mother Teresa, "Do not wait for leaders. Do it alone, person to person." Other saintly words came from St. Teresa of Avila centuries ago, but are still relevant today. She said, "Christ has no body now on earth but yours: Yours are the only hands with which he can do his work, yours are the only feet with which he can go about the world, yours are the only eyes through which his compassion can shine forth upon a troubled world. Christ has no body on earth now but yours."

PART 3

Preparations for the Journey

CREATE YOUR CORNERSTONE
WITH SPACE, MONEY AND SUPPORT.

CHAPTER 7

Create Space

De-clutter your way to a new career. Make room for the new by literally getting rid of the old. You'll experience life-changing benefits by discarding non-essential items.

Feng Shui shows how "less is more." Feng Shui is the ancient Chinese study dating back 6,000 years ago, based primarily on Buddhism, Taoism and Confucianism. It integrates ecology, psychology, astronomy and astrology into the practice of living in balance with nature and energy.

Feng Shui experts describe how our personal energy must go out to every single item we own: we have to look at, store, clean, dust or repair all our possessions. To welcome anything new into our life, we must first have space and energy for it: The idea is to first create a vacuum; then allow the Divine to fill it.

De-cluttering can be difficult, so tackle the task when you feel most ambitious. Make it easier by breaking it down into six manageable steps. Many of these excellent suggestions were taken from *Confessions of an Organized Homemaker*, by Deniece Schofield.

1. Take an Inventory.

Walk around and ask yourself:

- What do I own?
- How much of it do I need?

> *"Today, all I ask is that you be open to allowing a creative, sacred space to come into your world. If you are, spirit will do the rest."*
>
> Sara Ban Breathnach, author of *Simple Abundance*

❦ How would I benefit from having fewer possessions? For example: reduce dust mites, create a calmer environment, be able to find things faster and have friends over without being embarrassed.

2. Gather Necessary Supplies

❦ Several large trash bags with handles

❦ Wastebaskets (rent a dumpster for huge jobs)

❦ Boxes and plastic containers in various sizes

❦ Masking tape, colored markers to label bags, boxes and containers

3. Decide How and Where to Start

❦ Contemplate ways to approach the job. Do you work best in small chunks of time – say twenty minutes per day – or longer, marathon sessions?

❦ Tend to work best alone? Or with a friend?

❦ Which room is most compelling?

❦ Tackle a project that will yield an immediate visual payoff.

4. Set a Goal and Stick To It

❦ For maximum efficiency, stay focused in one area. Avoid the temptation to flit from room to room, which makes you less productive.

❦ Make the process enjoyable with music and a scented candle.

❦ If the weather is wonderful, throw open the windows.

❦ Set a realistic goal. Be sure to reward yourself when you complete your goal. Take in a movie or go out to dinner.

5. Drill as You Sort and Discard

❦ This is the most difficult, yet crucial part. As you sort through your belongings, ask yourself:

- Do I use this anymore?
- Is this something I love?
- Do I need so many of these?
- Have I worn this in the past year?

Creative ways to ditch "Too Good To Toss" items

- Have a party. Ask each guest to choose something from your "collection box."

- Put items you want to discard at the end of your driveway. Attach a sign "Free to a good home."

- A friend from New York shared his unique book exchange. When someone on his block finishes a book, they set it out on the sidewalk: anyone who wants it just picks it up, reads it, and returns it to the sidewalk for the next neighbor.

❧ Gifts from loved ones tend to be trickiest to part with, since people typically express their love with presents. Can you commit to keeping the love, while you let go of the undesirable gift?

❧ Although tempting, it isn't fair to loved ones if you ditch their belongings without their consent. Offer them assistance, encouragement and motivation by holding a family garage sale where everyone gets to keep the money they earn on their stuff.

❧ The world is abundant. Trust you'll have the resources to replace any discarded item you might later need.

❧ Discarded items can be distributed into one of eight marked boxes:

1. *Throw outs*
   Items damaged beyond repair.

2. *Hand-me-downs*
   Remain guilt free by passing family heirlooms down to siblings or kids.

3. *Charitable donations*
   Select your favorite. Remember to request a slip for tax time.

4. *Consignment shops*
   Check yellow pages for location.

5. *Garage sale*
   Hold your own or donate to church/ community sale.

6. *Recyclables*
   Newspapers, cans, bottles.

7. *Hazardous waste*
   Check with city hall for collection dates for paint, old medicine, etc.

8. *Questionables*
   Store items you don't use often in a box. Label the box with a 6-month "expiration date." If you haven't used or thought about the contents in six months, let it go.

Hoarding unused possessions takes energy, space and is selfish. Pass these items onto someone who can use them. It feels great.

6. Do it Daily

- De-clutter ten to fifteen minutes each day.

- Sort mail immediately and toss discards in recycle bin.

- For every new item that enters the house, strive to take out one old item.

Time as Space

While having lunch with an old college friend, our conversation turned to "home parties," those events where neighbors, friends and family are invited to someone's house to buy candles, clothes, kitchen gadgets, cosmetics, toys or other items they may not need or even want. My friend Rachel screamed, "I hate those parties! I tell my friends, if you need money, fine, I'll write you a check. If you want to socialize, great, let's meet for lunch. Just don't invite me to your home parties. I won't come!"

Her lesson was simple yet profound. We are in control of how we spend our time. Yes, we may get invited to things we don't want to attend and yes, it is awkward (for about two seconds) to say, "Sorry, I don't attend home parties." Yet how smart is it to spend two to three hours at something we despise?

Choose Commitments Wisely

Your career search will take both time and energy, so start choosing commitments wisely. Time is the most valuable commodity you have: be mindful of your minutes. Ann Richards, the former governor of Texas said, "We get in life what we are willing to demand." Demand to spend your time wisely.

Questions to Contemplate:

1. *In order to carve out time and energy for my career quest, what can I say no to this year?*

   ⮞ Home parties?

   ⮞ Being Cub Scout leader for the 4ᵗʰ year in a row?

   ⮞ Serving on six different church committees?

   ⮞ Overtime at the job?

   ⮞ Television?

   ⮞ Housecleaning? Cooking every night? Cleaning?

2. *What steps can I take this week to eliminate one chore I despise?*

3. *Can I kill two birds with one stone by choosing volunteer work that allows me to simultaneously develop my skills?*

A Space of One's Own

In the beginning, there was a plan. My handyman husband was going to build himself a simple garage to store bikes, gardening tools and cars. In the end, this simple plan evolved into a three-stall garage with a gorgeous, sunny, heated, air-conditioned, carpeted loft workspace above it. Neighbors nicknamed it the Garaje Mahal (rhymes with Taj Mahal).

This loft is mine, all mine. It's my sacred space where I work, write and see clients for

> *"It is only when we truly know and understand that we have a limited time on earth and that we have no way of knowing when our time is up- that we will begin to live each day to the fullest, as if it was the only one we had."*
>
> *Elisabeth Kubler Ross*

consultations. It is 700 square feet of heaven, and it started with a dream.

My husband received a divine vision and was led to construct the loft for me even before I knew what I'd use it for. Our credo became, "Build it – and the career will come." And my career did come. During the next three years as my husband built the loft, I gradually built my writing and consulting career. One month after I left my corporate job the loft was ready. In the words of Joseph Campbell, "If you have a sacred place, and use it, take advantage of it, something will happen."

You might not be able to swing a loft of your own right now, or even want one, but ask yourself what would most help your career exploration right now. A desk and a phone line of your own? File cabinets or bookshelves? A comfortable chair and quiet space to meditate? Studio space to create in?

Miraculous things can and do happen when a person claims a room of their own.

RECOMMENDED READING

- *Feng Shui- Harmonizing Your Inner and Outer Space* by Zaihong Shen
- *Wind and Water* by Carole Marcus Hyder
- *Organizing from the Inside Out: The Foolproof System for Organizing Your Home, Your Office and Your Life.* by Julie Morgenstern
- *Confessions of an Organized Homemaker The secrets of uncluttering your home and taking control of your life.* by Deniece Schofield

CHAPTER 8

Financial Foundation

Budgets, Bill Paying and Money Autobiographies
Money will play a practical and significant role in your career quest. Learn to make it a friend, not a foe.

Money Beliefs

In chapter one, you examined your core life beliefs. Now it's time to analyze your money beliefs. In her book, For Richer, Not Poorer, financial educator Ruth Hyden states, "Money beliefs are internalized emotional responses to a past [often negative] experience. Money beliefs – like core life beliefs – are significant because they control our thoughts, expectations, choices, behavior and outcomes."

> *"We are all richer than we think we are."*
>
> *Michel de Montaigne*

Hayden shares this example: Kate, a married woman, left all financial decisions to her husband because her core money belief was, "Men take care of money and women take care of relationships." But this money belief and resulting behavior didn't work well for Kate or her husband. So Kate chose to rewrite her belief to: "Women can competently handle money matters and men can be responsible for taking care of relationships." This revised money belief, and the resulting change in behavior is working much better for Kate and her husband.

Visualization

Gayle Rose Martinez, a financial counselor from Wisconsin uses this scenario to help her clients get at their core money beliefs.

> *"Imagine the ocean is God's source of financial abundance. You are free to take as much as you want. The amount you take for yourself will not diminish the supply for others, because God's abundance is infinite, never ending. There are no rules or limits. Now take a moment, close your eyes and visualize the bucket you'll use to collect your abundance.*
>
> *Is it large or small? Do you go back for refills or fill up just once? The container you choose and how much you take speaks volumes about your basic beliefs. A small sand bucket says, "I'm only entitled to a small amount, whereas a large dump truck with a continuous feeding hose proclaims, "I eagerly accept God's abundance!"*

"For the love of money is a root of all kinds of evil."

Timothy 6:10

"You cannot serve both God and money."

Matthew 6:24

"A faithful man will be richly blessed, but one eager to get rich will not go unpunished."

Proverbs 28:20

Suze Orman, financial advisor and author of three best selling books on personal finance states, "When it comes to money, I deeply believe that the obstacles that keep us from having more are rooted in the emotional, psychological and spiritual conditions that have shaped our thoughts. What we have begins with what we think."

What are your thoughts about money? Do you have conflicting beliefs? Maybe you have days when you trust God's abundance while other times you worry there won't be enough. Perhaps you question if it's even acceptable to have wealth, because of the Bible's multiple warnings. (see sidebar)

It is wise to be vigilant about your relationship with

money, but understand that money itself is neutral. It's neither good nor bad; money simply represents how our society has agreed to exchange labor for goods and services.

Living a spiritual life does not have to equal being poor. As a spiritual steward of God's abundance, imagine the work you could do. Feed the hungry, build homes for the homeless, fund scholarships, support medical research. The possibilities are endless. Be open to God's riches and commit to using money wisely.

Money Autobiography

Maria Nemeth is a psychologist, financial educator and author of The Energy Of Money. Maria encourages people to examine their relationship with money by writing a money autobiography.

Journal your answers to her questions
Past

> *1. What was your family's financial situation when you were born?*

_____

_____

_____

_____

> *2. How old were you when you first learned about money?*

_____

_____

_____

_____

3. *Did your father or mother teach you about money? What did they say?*

_____

_____

_____

_____

4. *Were you encouraged to save money?*

_____

_____

5. *How did you spend your first paycheck?*

_____

_____

_____

_____

6. *Do you remember ever losing money? How did you and others react?*

_____

_____

_____

_____

7. *During your childhood and adolescence, was there enough money to cover basic needs such as food, shelter and clothing? If not, how does the threat of poverty haunt you today?*

_____

_____

_____

_____

Current day

1. If you had to describe your relationship with money as a personal relationship, would you say it was generous and trusting, or possessive and mistrusting?

_____

_____

_____

2. In which areas of your life are you generous?

_____

_____

_____

3. What, or who do you refuse to spend money on? Why?

_____

_____

_____

_____

4. Is your spending in alignment with your values? List your values.

_____

_____

_____

_____

5. Name one thing you want to change about your spending.

_____

_____

_____

_____

Future

1. *What do you want your finances to be like ten years from now?*

_____

_____

_____

2. *What do you most want to accomplish with your money*

_____

_____

_____

3. *How will the world benefit from your abundance?*

_____

_____

_____

4. *When you are dead, what do you want people to say about the relationship you had with your money?*

_____

_____

_____

5. *Do you feel compelled to leave a significant inheritance? To whom and why? How much is enough?*

_____

_____

_____

_____

> *If a man has money, it is usually a sign, too, that he knows how to take care of it."*
>
> *Edgar Watson Howe*

Respect Money

Suze Orman tells us there is a direct correlation between money and respect. "Respect attracts money, disrespect repels money. Money is a living entity, and it responds to energy exactly the same way you do. It is drawn to those who welcome and respect it. If you are respectful of your money and do what needs to be done with it, you will become like a magnet, attracting more and more money to yourself."

Exactly how does a person show respect for money? Balance your checkbook every month. Become financially literate: enroll in a financial planning course, consult with a knowledgeable financial planner, invest wisely and read books on personal finances. Be responsible with your income and make conscious choices about your purchases.

Gratitude

It's easy, terribly easy, to take the most important things in life for granted: health, family, love, friends, freedom, faith. Acknowledge and give thanks every day for the multitude of blessings in your life. Thank the Creator for the love of family, a well-stocked pantry, a decent education, a reliable car, a warm, cozy house, healthy kids...

the list is endless. In the words of Melodie Beattie, "Gratitude unlocks the fullness of life. It turns what we have into enough... It can turn a meal into a feast, a house into a home, a stranger into a friend. Gratitude makes sense of our past, brings peace for today and creates a vision for tomorrow."

Give Back

Many religions teach tithing, namely giving back 10% of our income to help those less fortunate. Robert T. Kiyosaki, author of *Rich Dad/Poor Dad* says, "When you create wealth, it is your responsibility to return it to society." And although it defies logic, when we donate willingly to charities, the departed money makes room for abundance to flow back in again. Give and you shall receive – over and over again.

Budgets: Practical Suggestions

Many years ago, I told my friend, "I can't stand my job. I want to quit!" She replied in her usual helpful, practical manner, "Have you figured out how much you need to cover your monthly expenses?" An embarrassing silence followed. I didn't have a clue!

In retrospect, I realized that by not examining my finances, I was giving myself permission to stay stuck in a job I hated. Unconsciously I knew if I started looking at and resolving my financial matters, I might actually have to take a risk. I had to suffer awhile longer, and become absolutely miserable before I was ready to face my fears and make a career change.

So how badly do you want a passionate career? Do you want to pursue it now, or suffer awhile longer? If you are ready to build a bridge to a better, richer life, it's time to lay your financial foundation. It might not be easy, but it is necessary.

Getting Started

To compute what it costs to live each month, dig up at least six months worth of your canceled checks, credit card bills, ATM and checking account statements... anything that will give you an accurate picture of where your money goes. Grab a pad of paper, calculator and pencil and get comfortable. This will take time, energy and a firm commitment on your part.

On one sheet, write down all your current monthly expenses.

Break down items you pay quarterly or semi-annually into monthly averages.

For example if you pay $300 for car insurance twice a year: $300 + $300 = $600 per year
$600 divided by 12 (months) = $50 per month

Let this form guide you.

EXPENSES

Home Expenses

$_____ Rent/mortgage

$_____ Home upkeep, repairs

$_____ Home insurance

$_____ Utilities (Gas, lights, phone, water, trash, cable/internet)

$_____ Groceries

$_____ Lunches at work

$_____ Laundry and paper products

$_____ Lawn care

Family

$ _____ School tuition

$ _____ Alimony/Child support

Automobile Expenses

$ _____ Car payment

$ _____ Insurance

$ _____ License plates

$ _____ Gas

$ _____ Repairs and maintenance

Health / Medical

$ _____ Medical Insurance

$ _____ Dental Insurance

$ _____ Co-pays – Deductibles

$_____ Prescription drugs

$_____ Non-prescription drugs

$ _____ Out-of-pocket expenses

$ _____ Contact lenses, glasses

Entertainment & Gifts

$ _____ Movies

$ _____ Golf

$ _____ Sporting events

$ _____ Meals out

$ _____ Weddings/showers

$ _____ Birthdays

$ _____ Holidays

$ _____ Anniversary

$ _____ Graduations

Personal Items

$ _____ Clothing

$ _____ Shoes

$ _____ Uniforms

$ _____ Coats

$ _____ Undergarments

$ _____ Dry cleaning

$ _____ Jewelry

$ _____ Haircuts

$ _____ Manicures

$ _____ Shampoos, conditioner, beauty aids

$ _____ Health club membership

$ _____ Massages

Pet Expenses

$ _____ Veterinary check ups

$ _____ Food

$ _____ Kennels

Charitable Contributions

$ _____ Church, charities, fundraisers

Professional expenses

$ _____ Organizations, licenses

$ _____ Tuition, classes, lessons

$ _____ Books, magazines, newspapers

$ _____ Miscellaneous, unplanned emergencies

$ _____ **EXPENSE TOTAL**

On another sheet of paper, list all your financial debts. Include family or friends you owe money to, as well as financial institutions.

$ _____ Who do you owe money to?

$ _____ What is your balance and interest rate for each debt?

On another sheet, write down all your current monthly income. Break down items you receive quarterly or semi-annually into monthly averages.

MONTHLY INCOME

$ _____ Net income (paycheck after taxes)

$ _____ Predictable bonuses

$ _____ Social security or disability

$ _____ Rental income

$ _____ Retirement/ pension fund

$ _____ Alimony or child support

$ _____ Miscellaneous

$ _____ **INCOME TOTAL**

FINAL ANALYSIS

$ _____ **EXPENSE TOTAL**

$ _____ **INCOME TOTAL**

$ _____ **DIFFERENCE**

Compare your monthly expenses with your monthly income. What do the numbers tell you? Which category do you fall under?

Category 1: Spending less than I make

Category 2: Spending as much as I make

Category 3: Spending more than I make

Category 1

Start to pay off credit cards, bank loans, car loans or any other personal debt you've accrued. Build up your savings account as a financial cushion for your career quest. Consider meeting with a financial planner to discuss ways to invest your discretionary income and prepare for your future.

Category 2

Decide for yourself, "Where do I really want to spend my money?" Then use the money saving suggestions below to find ways to spend less. Apply these savings towards your debts. Soon you'll be building a savings account to support your journey to passionate work.

Category 3

Cut up those credit cards! When you spend more than you make, it leads to a spiral of debt, weighing you down, wearing you out and handcuffing you to a job you dislike. Be brave. Face your debt head on. Consider working with a financial counselor to negotiate a realistic payment structure for creditors. A financial counselor can give advice on a consolidation loan, help you explore ways to increase your income and find areas to reduce expenses.

"Why is there so much month left at the end of the money?"

Anonymous

FINANCIAL RESOURCES

National Foundation for Consumer Credit

Comprehensive financial services provided for individuals and families, debt management services

and information on buying a home.
Most services are free.
Toll free phone 1-800-388-2227
Website www.nfcc.org

These organizations typically have financial
counselors on staff. Check your business phone
directory for local listings.

Lutheran Social Services
Catholic Charities
Jewish Family and Children's Services

Debtor's Anonymous
Information and support groups for compulsive
spenders.
Phone 781-953-2753   Website
www.debtorsanonymous.com

Save

After your debts have been paid off, take a look
at your finances and set a savings goal. Financial
counselors advise having 3-6 months of living
expenses saved before quitting a job. How
much can you save every paycheck to build your
career transition cushion? Every dollar saved
helps you move closer to your goal of passionate
work. Use the tips below to stretch your dollars,
so there's more to save.

Money saving suggestions

General

- Join a buyers club and buy in bulk
- Avoid browsing as a hobby. Shop only when you truly need something.
- Try factory outlets, consignment and discount

stores as well as garage/estate sales.

- Pay bills on time to avoid finance charges.

- Barter/trade services. "I'll cut your hair if you replace my faucet. "

- Get a lower premium on your insurance by agreeing to a higher deductible. Pay annually for the lowest cost.

Food

- Grow a garden. Fresh food, fresh air, plus exercise.

- $3.00 for a cup of coffee?! Brew your own at home.

- Bring your lunch to work 3-4 days a week.

- Grocery shop only once a week. Plan a menu, stick to your list, shop on a full stomach and leave the kids at home.

- Use coupons and buy generic brands.

- Check day old bakery items. Freeze surplus.

- Purchase less expensive proteins: eggs, cheese, soy, beans and legumes.

Residential Cost Reductions

- Use a clothes line.

- Insulate your hot water heater and check the temperature. Most are set at 140° F, but you may not need it that hot.

- Run only full loads of laundry and dishes. Dishwashers use up to 14 gallons of hot water per load.

- Do any home repairs you're capable of. Wallpaper and paint with help from a handy friend.

- Replace vacuum cleaner bag frequently.

- Lower the thermostat to 55 at night and during the day when you're gone.

- Check ductwork for air leaks once a year.
- Turn off lights when leaving a room.

Car Care

If you need a new car, buy the most fuel-efficient car of the size and make you want. Consider purchasing a car at least six months to one year old, but have a reliable mechanic do a thorough, diagnostic check.

Practice Preventative Maintenance:

- Oil changes every 3,000 miles
- Tune ups every 5,000 miles
- Tires balanced, aligned, inflated to proper pressure
- Check fluids and filters regularly
- Spark plugs checked every 10,000 miles
- Regular car wash and wax to prevent rust
- Recommended gasoline octane and oil grade

"That man is richest whose pleasures are the cheapest."

Henry David Thoreau

Entertainment

- Vacations don't have to be expensive. Borrow a friend's cabin for a week or go camping.
- When you do travel, work through a good travel agent for lowest rates.
- Trade babysitting services with neighbors.
- Visit the dollar movie theatres.
- Bike or walk around the lake. It's free and the people-watching is great!
- Don't dine out at expensive restaurants. Host a potluck, where everyone contributes food and drinks.
- Watch for free community or church events: concerts in the park, ice cream socials, parades, classes or demonstrations.
- Join a book club. Check out books at the library.

Financial Advice for Entrepreneurs

Scott Simpson, a successful financial planner from Minneapolis said, "I support people who are willing to take great risks for a life that will be better, richer. People who start their own company tend to have maximum passion, but also maximum risk. I recommend people have at least 3-6 months of money tucked away to live on before they quit their jobs. And it's best if they can start their business while they're still employed."

Simpson explains that it may take up to five years for a new business to turn a profit, so he encourages clients to work at their new business part-time, say nights and weekends, while they still have income from their day jobs. Simpson adds, "It's crucial to have a mentor to meet with on a regular basis for advice, direction and support, especially in the beginning."

Faith Fills in the Gaps

Dare to dive in and dig yourself out of debt. Pay off bills, respect and appreciate your money and be open to God's abundance. Some may be forced to leap before their financial cushion is complete in their eyes. Perhaps it's God's way of teaching faith. Julia Cameron, author of *"The Artists Way"* writes, "Leap and the net will appear." Trust there will be enough to cover your basic needs and there will be.

RECOMMENDED READING

- *Think and Grow Rich*   by Napoleon Hill
- *Creating Money— Keys to Abundance* by Sanaya Roman and Duane Packer
- *50 Simple Things You Can Do to Improve Finances*   by Ilyce R Glink

- *The Truth About Money*   by Ric Edelman
- *Bonnie's Household Budget Book Essential Guide for Getting Control of Your Money*   by Bonnie Runyan McCullough
- *The Energy of Money — A Spiritual Guide to Financial and Personal Fulfillment* by Maria Nemeth, Ph.D.
- *How to Turn Your Money Life Around A Money Book for Women*   by Ruth Hayden
- *The Courage to Be Rich*   by Suze Orman
- *Creating a Life of Material and Spiritual Abundance*   by Suze Orman
- *The Road to Wealth*   by Suze Orman
- *Everything you Need to Know In Good Times and Bad Times*   by Suze Ormans
- *9 Steps to Financial Freedom*   by Suze Orman
- *Money Came By The House The Other Day A Guide to Christian Financial Planning* by Robert W. Katy

CHAPTER 9

Support Systems

Life is difficult. No doubt, your career quest, at times, will be difficult. Emotions will run the gamut from thrill and excitement to fear and trepidation. There will be obstacles to overcome and spiritual lessons to learn and integrate. But you are not alone and you don't have to face these challenges by yourself. Others want to help and support you in achieving your mission. Barbara Sher, author of *Wishcraft*, wrote, "What you have to do in this world you cannot do alone. Every successful human enterprise is a collaboration – a drawing together of diverse resources and energies to achieve a single end." United is how you'll make your mission happen.

"The smartest thing I ever said was, "Help me."

Anonymous

Asking for and accepting help sounds simple, yet for many it's complex. When we can't do something on our own, and need help, we are vulnerable. In America – where independence rules – relying on someone for assistance is often considered a sign of weakness. On top of these societal messages about doing it yourself, some people have to contend with negative family-of-origin messages about accepting help.

Use the questionnaire on the next page to assess your 'ability to accept help' quotient.

1. In my parents/guardians' home, I learned early on it wasn't OK to ask for help.   T   F

2. Teachers/students teased me when I asked for assistance in school.   T   F

3. When people do offer me help, I usually decline their offer.   T   F

4. I feel it's important to do most everything myself.   T   F

5. People say I'm extremely self-sufficient.   T   F

6. I've gotten into predicaments at work because I didn't ask for help.   T   F

7. When others ask for help, I think less of them.   T   F

8. When faced with health issues, I rarely call my doctor for advice.   T   F

9. One or both of my parents felt asking for help was a sign of weakness.   T   F

10. Friends have commented or joked about my inability to accept help.   T   F

"Like the body that is made up of different limbs and organs, all mortal creatures exist depending upon one another."

Hindu Proverb

Tally Your Trues

8-10   Accepting help is extremely difficult for you. See upcoming tips to enlighten your attitude.

4-7   You are frequently tempted to go it alone. Resist the temptation and let others help now and then.

1-3   Good for you! You can accept help when you need it.

Resist The Temptation To Go It Alone.

1. Recite this affirmation daily. *"I'm entitled to help on my career quest. The world is full of kind people who will support me."*

2. Enlist the help of family and close friends. Tell them you are learning to accept help and ask them for support and encouragement. Start small and ask for little favors. Eventually build up to larger ones.

3. There's a Scottish Proverb, *"Give and take makes good friends."* The ebb and flow of give and take keeps you connected and balanced. If you never take or accept, it throws off the natural balance between friends.

4. Consider counseling if you can't work through this on your own.

Supportive Friends Vs. Wet Blankets

"Negative people are vampires who keep going by sucking the life out of other people."

Mary Hirsch

It's important to identify people in your life you can count on for support. It's also crucial to name those you can't count on. According to Julia Cameron, author of *The Artist's Way*, people who throw cold water on you and your ideas are called "Wet Blankets – or W.Bs for short. Her advice is to avoid W.B.s as much as possible.

How can you tell supportive friends from W.Bs? Easy! Share your future goals and dreams, then watch their reactions. Supportive friends will be positive, affirming, hopeful and helpful. They'll say things like:

• Tell me more.

• I'd love to see you make better use of your talents.

• Life is short. Go for it!

- How can I help you?

- Keep me posted, ok?

W. B.s will come across negative, skeptical, fearful and perhaps shaming. Their comments will sound like:

- Don't be so unrealistic.

- Are you crazy?

- I don't understand you. Why can't you just settle for what you have, like the rest of us?

- I'm scared to death just thinking about your plans.

- How can you even consider quitting? Don't you know jobs are hard to come by these days?

Make a conscious commitment to spend more time with supportive friends, and less or no time with Wet Blankets.

Name supportive friends and family

_____

_____

_____

_____

Name Wet Blankets to avoid

_____

_____

_____

_____

Speak Up

People love to help. Let them know what you need and when. Naturally you'll want to express your gratitude and return the favor at some point.

When requesting help, be as specific as possible:

"Honey, I need two hours of uninterrupted, quiet writing time this weekend. Can you take the kids to the park Saturday afternoon?"

"I just bought a new computer and I could use help setting it up. Can you swing by either Tuesday or Wednesday night this week and give me a hand?

"Would you introduce me to your friend who owns the art gallery?"

> *"Actions, not words, are the true criterion of the attachment of friends."*
>
> George Washington

Shift in Friendships

As you proceed on your career quest, you'll no doubt influence others. You'll serve as a role model to friends and acquaintances seeking to make changes in their own lives. Your choices may give them the courage they need to take risks themselves.

Or the complete opposite may happen. There may be friends who will be frightened or intimidated by your decisions. Don't take it personally when those who are consumed with fear drift away. Trust that for every friend who goes away, one or two more will arrive who are more compatible with your evolving life.

Some souls, such as family and our closest friends, have contracted spiritually to stay with us our entire lifetime. Others may enter our life for shorter periods and leave when their purpose with us has been completed. Honor the ebb and flow in your relationships and pray for the discernment to know which ones to hang onto and which ones to let go of.

Self-Care As Support

You'll encounter change, chaos, uncertainty and lack of control on your career quest. But one thing you can control is how well you take care of yourself. If you treat your body well, you'll be in a better position to handle stress. Which areas can you improve upon?

Sleep

Most adults need 7-8 hours of sleep each night, yet studies show many Americans get only 6. If you're nodding off in the afternoon, hit the sack one hour earlier. You'll enjoy the difference.

Exercise

Health experts recently upped the exercise goal to one hour every day, but even 45 minutes, 4-5 times per week is good. Join a health club. Walk the dog after dinner. Take the kids for a bike ride. Make exercise fun by participating in a sport you enjoy.

Drinking/Eating

Drink 6-8 glasses of water a day. Limit caffeine intake, especially if you're jittery by nature or have trouble sleeping. Herbal teas are a pleasant substitute. If you are battling depression, eliminate or reduce alcohol consumption: it's a depressant. Limit fast food, take a daily multivitamin and strive to eat the recommended number of servings from the 6 major food groups:

Food group	Servings per day
Bread, rice, cereal, pasta	6-11
Vegetables	3-5
Fruits	2-4
Milk, yogurt, cheese	2-3
Meat, poultry, fish, eggs, dry beans, nut	2-3
Fats, oils	Consume sparingly

Balance

All good things in moderation: a well-rounded day contains work and play, exercise and relaxation, solitude and socializing.

Fresh Air

Let Mother Nature nurture you by spending time outdoors. Take a walk. Hike through the woods. Sit on a beach or walk along the shore. Watch the sunrise or catch a sunset.

Do something good for yourself every day. Self-love is not selfish, it just means you are important and your needs count, too. Surround yourself with people who respect you, treat you well and support you in achieving your life goals.

PART 4

Dealing with Demons

OVERCOME FEARS AND EMBRACE SUCCESS

Facing Fears

Shortly after I quit my job, I was hit by a tidal wave of fear. "What if my business fails? How will I feed and clothe my three growing kids? What an irresponsible mother I am! Why was I foolish enough to think I could do this?"

I wondered where this all-consuming fear was coming from. The answer came – of all places – in a fortune cookie that read, "Fear is the root of all evil." Suddenly I understood where these dark, survival fears were coming from: the devil himself! What better way for this evil entity to keep me stuck than to fill my head and heart with worries about my children's welfare.

> "And the day came when the risk it took to remain tight in the bud was more painful than the risk it took to blossom."
>
> *Anais Nin*

This type of limiting fear is not from the Divine. It's a powerful weapon from the dark side that seeks to prevent people from living the full life God intended for them. Fear keeps us from shining, can erode our initiative and confidence, and it separates our hearts from the Creator.

Fear goes hand in hand with making life changes. Barbara Sher, author of *Wishcraft* writes, "There is nothing in this world worth doing that isn't going to scare you. There is only one way to live free of fear – and that is to live without hope, without change and without growth."

Is that how you want to live your life? Without hope,

without change, and without growth? Then don't let fear get the upper hand. Expect to be frightened on your career quest, but find ways to deal with it.

Dealing With Fear

Ancient Chinese wisdom states, "What you want to overcome, you must first of all submit to." The first step to overcoming fear is to submit to it. Open yourself up. Acknowledge and embrace it. Honor and listen to your fear.

Eleanor Roosevelt said fear was a powerful teacher. "Fear and resistance are often our call to action. You gain strength, courage and confidence by every experience in which you really stop to look fear in the face...you must do the thing you cannot do." Trust that your lessons here on earth are directly linked to your fears. There is no easy way around fear, but you can go through it.

Name That Fear

The first step in dealing with your fears is to name them. Circle every fear you are currently experiencing on your career journey.

Fear of:
- Failure
- Financial ruin
- Survival (not being able to provide for myself, my family)
- Success
- Losing control
- Change
- The unknown
- Judgement and criticism from others
- Rejection or abandonment

> *"Life shrinks or expands in proportion to one's courage."*
>
> *Anais Nin*

- Looking stupid
- Being inadequate
- List any other fears

_____

_____

_____

_____

Deeper Fears

Fear – like an onion – has many layers. For example, I had a fear of success, but it took me several years to realize it was based on a deeper, related fear of abandonment. I had an unconscious fear that was sabotaging my writing. My fear was this: "When I become a successful writer and publish my thoughts and beliefs, those closest to me will reject and abandon me." With time, therapy, support from friends and family and God's grace, I finally worked through it.

Once I uncovered the fear, brought it to my awareness and began dealing with this demon, it no longer had the same power over me. Granted, I still had a tough choice to make: stay silent, and keep in the good graces of friends and family, or take a chance, write this book and risk abandonment. I prayed for faith, grace and the discernment to make the right choice. Through prayer God revealed to me the right time to write and publish this book.

> *"We cannot escape fear. We can only transform it into a companion that accompanies us on all our exciting adventures."*
>
> *Susan Jeffers*

Reflection Questions

1. *Be willing to take fear to a deeper level. Unravel it. Instead of saying, "I fear change" ask yourself, "What about change do I fear?"*

95

_____

_____

_____

_____

2. *As you identify your deepest fears, list what you gain by having this fear. What purpose does your fear serve? What does it allow you to avoid in life?*

_____

_____

_____

_____

3. *Is the fear truly yours or does it belong to someone else? As with core beliefs, you can respectfully, prayerfully send back what isn't yours.*

_____

_____

_____

_____

Three-Stepper

You can deal with limiting fears with this three-step approach.

1. Name the fear

2. Rank the chances of it happening

3. Create 5-10 options or solutions to handle the problem

Example

1. Name the fear.

*I fear my business will fail and I won't
be able to feed my kids.*

2. Rank the chances of it happening
   *Fifty percent of all new businesses fail,
   so I give my business a 50% chance of failing.*

3. Create five options or solutions to handle
   the problem.

   If my business fails I can still feed my kids by:

   - *waiting tables at a place where I can
     earn tips and bring home food.*
   - *going to the food shelf*
   - *taking my kids to my relatives*
   - *applying for food stamps*
   - *growing a large garden*

*Now it's your turn.
Repeat the 3-step process for each fear that surfaces.*

1. What fear do you have about your career quest?

_____

_____

_____

2. Rank the odds of that happening.

_____

_____

_____

3. If it did happen, what are 5-10 ways to deal with it.

> "A man's doubts and
> fears are his worst
> enemies."
>
> *William Wrigley, Jr.*

_____

_____

_____

False Evidence Appearing Real

Have you heard of the acronym for FEAR? "False Evidence Appearing Real." How many times have you feared something bad might happen and it never did? Think of all that wasted energy worrying over something that never happened. And even if the unthinkable does happen, you'll be halfway to handling it since you already brainstormed solutions.

Thoughts Create Reality

Our thoughts are one of the most powerful forces we have. Be mindful of what you dwell on and fill your head with. Strive for my 90/10 rule: strive to think positively 90% of your day, and limit negative thoughts to under 10% of your day. If you need help limiting yourself, set a timer for ten minutes. When it dings, you're done thinking negatively!

Move Forward by Looking Back

Think about the times in your life when you have successfully conquered fear. Did you go away to college by yourself? Move to a different city? Start a new job? Ask someone out? Get married? Have children? Learn to drive?

"Taking a new step, uttering a new word, is what people fear most."

Fyidor Dostoyevski

What did you have then that helped you overcome your fear? What would help you now? Support from friends? Prayer? Optimistically visualizing a positive outcome? Upbeat self-talk? Writing affirmations? Do whatever it takes to keep moving on your career quest. Even baby steps are good.

Perfectionism is Poison

When you were learning to walk, you stumbled, staggered, fell, bumped your head on the coffee table and landed on your bottom. But you got back up and kept trying until you finally mastered walking. No one expected you as a baby to walk

Facing Fears

> *"To live a creative life, we must lose our fear of being wrong."*
>
> *Joseph Chilton Pearce*

perfectly on your first try. Likewise, when trying something new as an adult, don't expect perfection on the first try. Cut yourself some slack. Writer Anne Lamott cautions, "Perfectionism is the voice of the oppressor, the enemy of the people. It will keep you cramped and insane your whole life."

Consider failure a great fertilizer for future accomplishments. Learn to lower your standards, at first, allowing plenty of room for mistakes. We learn by doing, there is no other way.

Celebrate Attempts

A friend of mine, Patsy Keech tells the story of her young son who tried out for the school play, but unfortunately didn't make the cut. As an educator and encouraging mom, she decided it was important to honor his brave attempt regardless of the outcome, so she took him out to eat at his favorite restaurant. Do like Patsy does: celebrate your attempts in life, even if you don't make the cut.

Sense of Humor

> *"She who laughs, lasts."*
>
> *Lilly Tomlin*

Bill Cosby says, "If you can laugh at it, you can survive it." Students chuckle when I share this story from my early freelance writing days. I had submitted an article to a local parenting publication and shortly afterwards the editor called saying, "We'd love to publish your piece, but your lead was pretty weak. Can you rewrite it?" Thrilled that she wanted to publish my piece, I eagerly blurted, "Sure, I can rewrite the lead. " After a moment of silence I asked, "By the way, what's a lead?"

In the words of Thomas Moore, "Humor allows us to entertain failure and inadequacy without being literally undone by them." Learn to laugh at yourself and you'll be one mental health step ahead of your peers.

First Aid Kit for Fear – 13 Lucky Tips

- Pray for grace, strength, persistence and wisdom
- Ask your guardian angel to protect you
- Dream about ways to overcome fear
- Sit with a friend and talk over your fears
- Laugh in the face of fear
- Journal about your fears
- Recite this daily affirmation: "The Creator is abundant and meets all my needs."
- Live in the moment. You only have to solve today's problems today.
- Write down your fear on a piece of paper, then burn it.
- Paint or draw a picture of yourself conquering fear.
- Think about a brave friend. Act like they would.
- Keep breathing.
- Take baby steps and celebrate small accomplishments.

If you live life to its fullest, fear will be your constant companion. Get used to it. Feel the fear; then do it anyway. Pray for grace and trust God to protect and support you on your journey. Recognize you are not alone: you have guides, God, friends and family. Dealing with fear won't be easy or enjoyable, but there are far greater discomforts. If you let fear limit your life, you'll suffer emotionally, spiritually and physically.

CHAPTER 11

Embracing Success

I teach a freelance writing course and ask students to visualize themselves as successful writers. Many run into blocks with this exercise. When they process afterwards, their comments, concerns and questions frequently reveal their fear of success.

"Failure I can handle. It's success that scares me the most. If I'm published, people will expect more. What if I don't have anything else in me? "

"If my book is successful then my life might change drastically! I like my life just the way it is."

"When I publish my opinion, people might disagree with me. I don't know if my skin is thick enough to handle hate mail from readers."

"If I become rich and famous, I'm afraid I'll turn into a nasty person."

"I'd be waiting for the other shoe to drop."

> *"Success seems to be largely a matter of hanging on after others have let go."*
>
> William Feather

These writers fear success because they have been conditioned to equate success with negativity: they assume bad things will happen to them when they become published writers, so they find creative ways to sabotage their writing success. I've seen writers:

1. Strive for weeks to land an assignment, then turn it down because of some lame reason.

2. Work diligently for years to complete a book, then never submit it for publication.

3. Accept an assignment from an editor, procrastinate until the last minute, then turn in the article late.

4. Take numerous creative writing courses, read multiple books on writing, but somehow never find time to write.

5. Refuse to submit work to anyone, because they fear it isn't perfect or they aren't good enough.

6. Let one little rejection letter crush their ego and stop them cold.

Shooting Yourself In The Foot

Self-sabotage, known in the mental health field as self-defeating behaviors, or SDBs for short, are ways we operate that work against – or even harm us. Milton Cudney and Robert Hardy co-wrote the book, *Self-defeating Behaviors: Free Yourself from the Habits, Compulsions, Feelings and Attitudes That Hold You Back.* They write, "A true self-defeating behavior is an action or attitude that once worked to help an individual cope with a hurtful experience, but that now works against the individual to keep him or her from responding to new moments of life in a healthy way." Shirley Rutherford, Minneapolis clinical psychologist says, "We develop self-defeating behaviors because they offer some kind of comfort or protection from a not-so-kind world. Self-defeating behaviors are learned behaviors that have somehow been reinforced. These behaviors work well enough to become entrenched in our lives, but they are never the best choice."

"The only thing that will stop you from fulfilling your dreams – is you!"

Tom Bradley

Here's An Example Of How SDBs Develop.

Rachel, a sophomore in high school, tries out for the softball team, but doesn't make the cut. She's angry, disappointed and slightly humiliated. Rachel goes home and wolfs down a dozen chocolate chip cookies, warm out of the oven. Rachel feels better temporarily, but eating a couple dozen chocolate chip cookies was not the best choice. Rachel could have:

1. Talked over her feelings with a close friend, family member or perhaps someone else that didn't make the team.

2. Gone for a walk or run to work out her frustration and anger.

3. Talked to the coach to find out why she was cut and elicit suggestions for how she could make the team next year.

4. Checked out other sports or school activities.

Self-defeating behaviors don't help a person achieve their goals, because SDBs are never *the best* solution. Self-defeating behaviors can lead to problems of their own. Imagine the health issues Rachel would experience if she handled every single rejection in life by eating a dozen chocolate chip cookies.

Self-defeating behaviors range in severity and can be classified into three categories physical, emotional and behavioral.

Physical

- Eating issues: overeating, bulimia, anorexia

- Abuse of alcohol, prescription or street drugs

- Smoking

Emotional

- Worrying/ anxiety

- Isolation, alienation

- Depression

Behavioral

- Gambling

- Procrastination

- Perfectionism

- Lack of risk-taking (always playing it safe)

- Compulsive behaviors (excessive hand washing)

- Hostility

- Conforming

Breaking The Cycle Of Self-Defeating Behaviors With These Steps

1. Identify the SDB you want to change.

2. Note when, where and with whom the behavior is practiced.

3. Create a list of healthier, alternate behaviors.

4. When you catch yourself in the act, break out of your rut by trying something, anything new from your list of healthy alternatives.

5. Record your success in a journal.

6. Reward yourself in a healthy way for the new behavior.

Example

1. *Overeating junk food.*

2. *Late at night after a hard day at work. When alone.*

3. *Walk the dog. Call a friend. Go to the health club. Have celery sticks and carrots cut*

up in the fridge. Eat veggies instead of junk.
Knit, crochet or read.

4. *Catch myself eating potato chips. Get up and*
    grab the carrot and celery sticks instead.

5. *Record success in my journal. 4 out of 5 nights*
    this week I did well.

6. *Treat myself to a movie out with friends*
    this weekend.

Expect improvements to be gradual and don't give up when you experience occasional setbacks. Just start over again. If your problem is severe (depression, eating disorders, anxiety attacks, drug or alcohol abuse) seek professional help.

Successful People Get a Bad Rap

Think of all the negative stereotypes you've heard about successful people. Successful people are:

- Selfish
- Con artists
- Money hungry
- Unethical
- Cheaters
- Obsessed
- Lonely
- Stingy/frugal

Can all those stereotypes possibly be true of every successful person in the world? Of course not! Look for successful people who are also generous philanthropists. The entertainment field has many philanthropic role models. Paul Newman donates a portion of profits from his Gourmet Food line to feed the hungry. Mia Farrow uses her financial wealth from acting to personally adopt, raise and nurture hard to place, handicapped children. Oprah Winfrey founded the *Angel Miracle Network* to channel her financial abundance to charitable organizations around the country. The late Dave Thomas, founder of Wendy's, used his abundance to fund adoption programs. Jerry Lewis is perhaps best known for his annual muscular dystrophy telethon.

Women especially have difficulty embracing success, due in large part to a "B" word (rhymes with "itch") that society likes to slap on prosperous females.

As mentioned in Chapter 8 on finances, religious organizations frequently send negative messages about success and money. While we certainly don't want to let money become our god, we must not equate a meaningful life of service with being destitute. Unlike people in religious orders who take a vow of poverty, we do not need to reject money to serve the Divine. Let me say that again: we do not need to reject money to serve the Divine.

Money itself is neutral – neither good or bad. It's the choices we make about money that take on moral implications. Do we hoard funds and waste money frivolously, or do we choose wisely and share our abundance with those less fortunate? It's your choice.

Make a commitment today to be generous with the money you manifest in the future. Trust yourself as a responsible steward and allow the Divine to work through you, in order to make the positive changes needed for those less fortunate.

Success Your Way

Forget society's definition of success and begin

to visualize your own version of success with a unique life that satisfies your heart's desires, your needs, preferences, quirks and interests. Use these reflection questions to warm up, then draw a picture or make a collage using words and images that paint a picture of your future successful life and career.

Reflection Questions For Your Successful Life

"You can have anything you want if you want it desperately enough. You must want it with an exuberance that erupts through the skin and joins the energy that created the world."

Sheila Graham

• *How many hours do you wish to work?*

_____

• *Do you work every day or just a few days each week?*

_____

• *Would a flexible schedule work best with your personal commitments?*

_____

• *Do you work from home or do you prefer a downtown office?*

_____

• *Are you working outdoors, indoors, or both, depending upon the weather?*

_____

• *What type of clothes are you wearing? Casual, dress up, or both?*

_____

• *Can you picture the type of service or product you are providing?*

_____

• *How much do you make per hour?*

_____

ᴥ *How are you freely channeling your creativity?*

_____

ᴥ *Are you working alone or with others?*

_____

ᴥ *Would you like to travel? Frequently or occasionally?*

_____

ᴥ *What hobbies do you now have time, money and energy for?*

_____

ᴥ *What charity work do you see yourself doing?*

_____

"Authentic success comes only after we have mastered failing better."

Sarah Ban Breathnach

ᴥ *How does this job improve your family's lifestyle?*

_____

ᴥ *What can you do, or buy, for extended family members and friends, now that you are financially well off?*

_____

Have Faith in Failure

If you want to be a success, have faith in your failures. Most successful people including writers, politicians, athletes, actors, actresses and business entrepreneurs have failed at some point in their life.

Did You Know?

- Twenty-three book publishers rejected the first Dr. Seuss book, written by Theodore Seuss Geisel.

- Michael Jordan was cut from his high school basketball team.

"Do not fear mistakes. There are none."

Miles Davis

- Henry Ford went broke five times before he finally succeeded with his car company.

- Before becoming president, Abraham Lincoln ran for and lost several political elections, battled bouts of depression and was rejected by the first woman he proposed to.

Successful people will naturally experience some failure on the way to a prosperous, accomplished life. To be successful, a person must take risks, and when a person takes risks, they automatically increase their odds of experiencing failure. But trust Mickey Rooney who says, "You always pass failure on the way to success."

If you want to succeed, make friends with failure. If you haven't had a good, conspicuous, cry-on-someone's shoulder failure recently, I feel sorry for you. It means you haven't stretched yourself or tried something new in an awfully long while. In my opinion, people who never attempt anything new fail by default, because they are living a confined, boring life.

Avoiding failure should never be your overriding goal. When taking risks and trying new behaviors, cut yourself a little slack and give yourself a lot of credit. It takes guts to risk failure. Have faith that each failure will bring you one step closer to success.

A Personal Story

About now you're probably thinking. "Easy for the author to say have faith in your failures. She's doesn't have a clue about real life."

I beg to differ. I share my story at this point in the book not to elicit feelings of sympathy, or to boast, but to help you grasp that I am a normal person who faced the same types of struggles you face right now. I experienced many ups and downs on my own career quest, but I kept going. A combination of hard work, helpful people, risk taking and Divine intervention led to my holy grail: finding work that I love.

In a nutshell, here's my story. My parents couldn't afford to send me to college – due in part to my dad's mental illness – so I applied for financial aid, took out a couple student loans and worked several jobs throughout my college years.

Next I got married, completed graduate school, landed a corporate job and had three kids over the next five years. In an effort to spend as much time as possible raising our kids, my husband and I worked opposite shifts for ten years while the kids were young.

In 1995, the roller coaster ride of setbacks and failures began. After thirteen years in corporate life, I took up freelance writing as a way to creatively express myself and make a difference in the world. My first fifty submissions to editors were rejected, but I kept going, determined to achieve success. After much trial, error, tears and consolatory ice cream, I did succeed, publishing numerous articles and eventually landing my own syndicated column.

> *"Only those who risk going too far will ever know far they can go."*
>
> Anonymous

After leaving the confines of a corporate job that was too small for my spirit, I started my own business and experienced a 75% cut in pay my first year. Then it was my husband's turn. He quit his job and took out a second mortgage to finance a business adventure that we ultimately lost our shirts on. While I wrote this book (which by the way was rejected by eighteen publishers) we tightened our family financial belt and lived off my income, our savings and my husbands retirement funds.

I have compassion for all my clients and readers who are challenged to let go of the given (namely a steady pay check and paid health insurance) in exchange for the unknown. The journey is far from easy, but having lived through it, I can assure you the reward of passionate work is worth it.

> *"Confidence comes with success. Success comes from persistence."*
>
> Bill Farmer

Failure As a Learning Tool

After thousands of failed attempts to light the first light bulb, Edison remarked, "I haven't failed. I've discovered 10,000 ways this doesn't work!." Failure can be a great way to gather information. When clients of mine interview for jobs, but get rejected, I encourage them to go back and ask the interviewer these questions:

- Who did get the job?
- Was it someone internal or external?
- Can you tell me what they had that I didn't have?
- Do I lack education, experience or skills?
- How was my attitude?
- What can I do to become a stronger candidate for this position in the future?

Failure and rejection are also great ways to test how bad you want something. Have you ever expressed a sigh of relief when you were turned down for something? There are times we go after things we honestly don't want.

But if you were rejected and still want it, hang in there. Be persistent and keep at it. Human resource professionals say it's not always the person most qualified who gets the job. Quite often it's the person who is most persistent, showing more passion and enthusiasm for the position than others.

Instead of staying down when you fail at something, get back up, brush yourself off, reassess and revise, and then move forward.

RECOMMENDED READING

- *Prospering Woman- A Complete Guide to Achieving the Full, Abundant Life* by Ruth Ross

- *Self-defeating Behaviors: Free Yourself from the Habits, Compulsions, Feelings and Attitudes That Hold You Back* by Milton Cudney and Robert Hardy

- *Get Out of Your Own Way* by Tom and Natalie Rusk

- *Why Can't I Get What I Want* by Charles Elliot

- *Self-traps- The Elusive Quest for Higher Self-Esteem* by William B. Swann, Jr.

PART 5

Spiritual Guidance

LEARN TO ACCESS DIVINE GUIDANCE

CHAPTER 12

Intuition

INner voice

INsight

INstinct

Entire books have been written on intuition, the ability to perceive things out of the natural range of our five senses. Intuition has frequently been called our sixth sense. Other cultures, like the Chinese and Hebrew, have rich symbols that seem to fully capture the essence of intuition. Our limited, linear language does not do justice to intuition, but it's what we have to work with.

Definitions of intuition include:

- Psychic perception or awareness
- Subjective knowing
- Sensation
- Power to discern the true nature of a person or situation
- Universal, intelligent life force that exists within everyone
- Deep wisdom

Who Has Intuition?

Everyone has intuition, but it's primarily associated with women for two reasons: society gives women permission to use intuition and women have traditionally been in touch with

> *"The intuitive mind is a sacred gift and the rational mind is a faithful servant. We have created a society that honors the servant and has forgotten the gift."*
>
> *Albert Einstein*

their feelings. Even though it's often called, "women's intuition," men have intuition, too. Over the years, I've witnessed more and more men honoring and applying intuition in their personal and professional lives. When a businessman says he based a decision on "a gut feeling," that's intuition at work. Men simply find it more sociably acceptable to call it something else.

Where Does Intuition Come From?

My simple answer is intuition comes from the Creator, but Echo Bodine, an internationally renowned psychic, spiritual healer and author gives a more detailed answer. "Intuition is that part of us that is connected to the divine." When our souls were created, the source that created us took a part of its energy and breathed eternal life into us. This part of us is commonly referred to as our Higher Self – or the God within."

Intuition has been described as a channel between this world and the next, providing a connection to the universal knowledge or consciousness that exists. Peter Shockey, a documentary filmmaker of supernatural phenomenon and the author of *Reflections of Heaven* writes, "I am convinced that He [God] has created an organized system for running the universe in both the physical and spiritual realm. He has provided us with tools and opportunities for communicating with Him and obtaining help and guidance when we need it."

Intuition is one of those powerful tools and, like a muscle, the more we use it the stronger it gets. Begin to honor, listen to and trust it. Intuition can provide concrete, practical help in your professional and personal life.

"Trust that still, small voice that says, "This might work and I'll try it."

Diane Mariechild

116

Red Light, Green Light

Since I'm a visual person, I use an intuitive process I call red light, green light. I break down daily decisions into simple questions with yes or no answers. Then I close my eyes, ask the question and wait to receive a red light or green light. In my mind's eye, I see a colored light. Red means no or stop, green means yes, or go ahead.

> *"The Kingdom of God is within you."*
>
> Jesus

- "Will this editor accept my column?"
  Green, yes.

- "Is that dress I liked on sale yet?" Red, no.

A yellow light indicates uncertainty. The answer might not be available to me for some unknown reason, or I may not have phrased the question simply enough.

For example:

"Should I buy gas today or is the price going down tomorrow?" I would get a yellow light until I reduced the question to, "Should I buy gas today?"

> *"I shut my eyes in order to see."*
>
> Paul Gauguin

Not everyone in the paranormal field distinguishes between intuition and psychic abilities. Some argue that it's a case of semantics, but Echo Bodine has a strong opinion. "Intuition and psychic abilities are not the same thing." Bodine feels everyone has intuition, whereas psychic ability is just one of many talents that a person can be blessed with. She states, "How much you've used these abilities in past lives will determine what your strong areas will be in this life."

Most psychics do agree that there are four distinct types of psychic gifts. Some people have only one type, while others may have a combination of two or more. Do any of these gifts feel familiar to you?

Four Psychic Abilities

1. **Clairvoyance: Clear Seeing**

   Clairvoyance is the gift of seeing visions, images and pictures. It's similar to watching a movie or cartoon strip, but instead of on a television or movie screen it is in your head.

2. **Clairaudience: Clear Hearing**

   Clairaudience is hearing clear, audible voices from some type of spirit realm.

3. **Clairsentience: Clear Sensing**

   Clairsentience is being able to sense information in the body. People with this gift are like psychic sponges, intuitively sensing and absorbing other people's emotions, thoughts and feelings. A clairsentient can often "feel" other people's health challenges in their own body.

4. **Claircognizance: Clear Knowing**

   Claircognizance is sure and certain knowing. People with this ability say it's like having a Divine computer disk in their head, giving them revelations, facts, insights, inspiration, foresight and ingenuity. Inventors often have this psychic ability.

Experiment with your intuition to get answers to major and minor life decisions. Pay attention to how your body responds to questions, situations and people. Remember, the more you use intuition, the stronger it gets. In the words of Johann Von Goethe, "Just trust yourself, then you will know how to live."

"These gifts I give to you and greater works shall you do."

Jesus

RECOMMENDED READING

> *"We need to be willing to let our intuition guide us, and then be willing to follow that guidance directly and fearlessly."*
>
> *Shakti Gawain*

- *Developing Intuition- A Practical Guide for Daily Life*   by Shakti Gawain
- *Second Sight*   by Judith Orloff, M.D.
- *A Still, Small Voice —A Psychic's Guide to Awakening Intuition*   by Echo Bodine
- *Awakening Intuition*   by Mona Lisa Schulz
- *Women's Ways of Knowing* by Belenky, Clinchy, Goldberger and Tarule

CHAPTER 13

Dreams

Dreams are a powerful source of spiritual guidance. Learn to recall, interpret and integrate them in your career and life journey.

Origins

The debate over where dreams come from is centuries old. Some say dreams come from our subconscious or unconscious mind, while many claim that God sends dreams. Others believe spirit guides, angels or deceased ancestors deliver dreams. The mystery about dream origins may never be solved (who knows – maybe everyone is right) but a more relevant question to ponder is, "Can dreams help us in our every day life?" Jeremy Taylor, dream researcher and author of *Where People Fly and Water Runs Uphill* says, "Yes! Dreams can indeed help us in our daily life." Here are five of his ten basic assumptions about dreams.

"Dreams are illustrations from the book your soul is writing about you."

Marsha Norman

1. All dreams come in the service of health and wholeness.

2. No dream comes just to tell the dreamer what they already know.

3. All dreams reflect an inborn creativity and ability to face and solve life's problems.

4. All dreams reflect society as a whole, as well

as the dreamer's relationship to it.

5. Working with dreams regularly will improve your relationship with friends, partners, parents, children and others.

Benefits Of Dreams

In many societies, shamans or healers use dreams to diagnose illness. Some cultures have used dreams to find game, predict the weather and prophesy the future. Psychotherapists started using dream work in their therapeutic sessions with clients around 1900. In her book *Living Your Dreams*, dream expert and psychologist Gayle Delaney states, "Your dreams are not senseless blitherings of the night. They offer you insight, understanding and inspiration. They serve a purpose and have a message. It's up to you to grab it." Dreams can help us understand, unwrinkle and resolve problems in life.

Striving for Dream Recall

If you don't remember your dreams, don't fret. Anyone seeking insight, clarity and guidance can easily learn to recall and interpret their dreams. Reasons vary as to why we lose touch with our dreams, but one current day culprit is the alarm clock: getting jolted out of bed does nothing for dream recall. Another reason why we might not remember our dreams is that we haven't been paying attention to them.

If you need help remembering your dreams, try this:

1. Decide wholeheartedly that you want to remember and understand your dreams. Remind yourself of this right before you fall asleep.

2. Upon awakening, lie still. If you have forgotten

your dream go back to the physical position you woke up in. Then ask yourself again, what was I dreaming?

3. Buy a dream journal and place it by your bed. Record your dreams when you wake up, even if it's in the middle of the night.

It should only take one or two nights of prompting before you remember your dreams.

Dream Incubation

When faced with challenging decisions on your career journey, sleep on it. The process of sleeping on a particular problem is called dream incubation. With practice and a few simple techniques, you can target dreams to resolve specific issues.

Author Gayle Delaney explains, "In this dream state, you have access to valuable information on the state of your mind, body and spirit. You also have access to insights on the nature of your relationship...as well as strengths and abilities you have not used." She explains that dreams provide an arena to screen test various possible future actions and compute their likely outcome.

Delaney's Seven-step Method for Dream Incubation *

1. **Choose the right night**
   Be sure you are not overly tired or under the influence of drugs or alcohol.

2. **Day notes**
   Take notes during the day describing your thoughts, feelings and efforts made to resolve the problem.

*rpt from Chapter 2, pages 23-26 from LIVING YOUR DREAMS REVISED AND EXPANDED
TION by Gayle M. Delaney Copyright (c) 1978, 1081, 1988 by Gayle M. Delaney, Ph.D.
inted by permission HarperCollins Publishers Inc.*

3. Incubation discussion

Write down the issue that you would like illuminated and answer these questions.

- ❧ What are the causes of the problem?
- ❧ Does living with the problem feel safer than resolving it?
- ❧ How would things be different if the problem were resolved?"

4. Incubation phase

Write one line clearly stating what you would like to understand about your problem.

For example:
"Help me understand my fear of success."

5. Focus

Repeat the phrase as you fall asleep. Imagine you are about to begin production of a dream scene that will answer your question.

6. Sleep

7. Awaken and record whatever is on your mind

Jot down any feelings and associations you can make.

> *"I realized that those who were most effective and inspiring were those who made a connection between their spiritual practice and their work in the world."*
>
> *Lance Brunner*

Delaney gives us this advice. "Expect your incubated dream to come the same night you ask for it, providing solutions you may not have considered. Some incubated dreams will have a soothing, almost healing effect; the very experience of the dream may change your mind or feeling in a way that helps resolve the conflict. Trust the dream producer within you to skillfully craft what is most helpful."

Interpreting Dreams

Unlocking or interpreting your dream will take time and energy. Since dreams are a private message to the dreamer, you will be the only one who can interpret your dreams. Discuss your dreams with friends or a therapist, but understand you are the only one who can make the correlations.

Most dreams are metaphorical or symbolic in nature; discovering who or what they resemble is the key to your interpretation. A dream dictionary can be a helpful guide, but interpretations vary depending upon the dreamer, his or her emotions and unique situation.

Trust your intuition and first association. Pay close attention to your feelings in the dream. Make a conscious choice to think about your dream during the day. Create a hypothesis about how the pieces fit together, and then test these insights in the real world. Process your dreams with friends and loved ones, but share only what feels comfortable. Remember, you are the final authority on your dream's meaning.

Many years ago in the thick of my career quest, I had the same dream every night. I was a passenger on an airplane that was about to crash. I looked up airplanes in several dream books and discovered airplanes have more than one meaning. One book said airplanes symbolize how a person moves through the mental aspects of their world. Another book indicated airplanes usually have something to do with risk taking.

The books and descriptions were somewhat helpful, but I was still having the dream night after night. So I asked for a follow-up dream that would explain the personal message more clearly. The next dream was similar to the others, but provided more details. First, my kids were on board with me. Second, I saw that the pilot was flying erratically. In my dream, I asserted myself by entering the cockpit and demanding that he pay more attention to what he was doing. And in this final dream, I saw that the airplane did make an emergency landing, but we escaped safely thanks to the efforts of the emergency workers on the ground.

For days I contemplated my follow up dream until the two meanings became clear. In order for me and my family to survive my career journey, I would need to learn to assert myself and speak up for what was right and I need to accept help along the way: Two major lessons I continue to work on today.

Stay open to the messages, insights and connections that your dreams provide. Allow them to illuminate your career quest.

RECOMMENDED READING

- *Where People Fly and Water Runs Uphill*
  by Jeremy Taylor

- *Living your Dreams*
- *In Your Dreams*
  by Gayle Delaney, Ph.D.

- *The Encyclopedia of Dreams*
- *Dreamwork for the Soul*
  by Rosemary Ellen Guiley

- *Dreamscaping*
  by Sanley Kripper and Mark Robert Waldman

- *The Dreamers Workbook*   by Nerys Dee

- *Conscious Dreaming*   by Robert Moss

CHAPTER 14

Angels, Spirit Guides, Past Lives

Angels

It is written in the Bible that angels have existed from the beginning of time, even before Adam and Eve entered the garden. "After the first humans were driven from Eden for having eaten of the Knowledge of right and wrong, the cherubims, which are one of the three orders of angels closest to God, stood guard at the east gate. Their fiery swords turned every which way to keep Adam and Eve from returning to eat also from the tree of Immortal Life." Genesis.

Meaning, Purpose and Appearances

"Nobody can conceive or imagine all the wonders there are, unseen and unseeable, in the world."

Francis P. Church

The word angel is derived from a Greek word that means messenger. Angels, divine messengers from God, are purportedly sent for three reasons:

1. To bring light, hope and inspiration to the world

2. To protect us

3. To light our path and show us the way

Many believe angels can come to us as voices, visions, signs, thoughts, and in our dreams. Angels might even work through our animals, when necessary. Those who have been allowed to see angels use words like "brilliant, radiant, and luminous" to describe them.

Saint Francisca, a fourteenth-century French saint had a guardian angel and was permitted to see his great beauty. She said he had long, curly blond hair and wore a floor-length robe that was either white, blue or red. His face was "whiter than snow, redder than the blush rose" and his eyes were always lifted to the heavens. His radiance was so luminous St. Francisca could read at midnight by his light. Once she took her angel by the hand and introduced him to her spiritual advisor, who miraculously saw him too.

> *"Every blade of grass has its Angel that bends over and whispers, "Grow. Grow."*
>
> The Talmud

Sophy Burnham, author of *Book of Angels* says there are three definitive markings of an angel appearance:

1. Their message is always one of hope.
   ("Fear not. Things will work out perfectly.")

2. They bring a sense of calm and peaceful serenity.

3. The person who experiences the angel visit is never quite the same afterwards.

Angels are different than ghosts. Ghosts are spirits of the dead, humans who have lived on this earth, whereas angels are not, and never have been human. As messengers of the Divine they are full of God's pure knowledge.

It doesn't matter if you can or can't see angels. Trust they are always with you to protect, inspire and light your way. Know you are never alone.

Spirit Guides/Personal Guides

I believe we have one or more spirit guides, also called personal guides. Author Char Margolis explains the purpose of these guides. "They are there to help us do the best we can with our lives, mainly by guiding us at certain times and protecting us from negative energies. They communicate with our soul in various ways; sending pictures in our heads, putting thoughts in our mind, or they can come through our dreams."

Our guides are not God; they are spirits, more like us. They may be souls who have lived before, but unlike angels, our guides don't know everything. They love us, want to help, protect and communicate with us. You can choose to accept or reject the advice of your guides, much like the counsel of a good friend, based on your free will, intuition, judgement and prayers.

I surmise we each have one or two spirit guides who contract to stay with us our entire lifetime. In addition we have other guides who visit us, based on the challenges we are facing or the work we are doing. I've never "seen" my guides, but I do sense their presence, especially when I write, hold counseling sessions with clients or participate in healing work. They also come when I'm lonely, depressed or confused.

It's been said that up until age two, children are able to see their spirit guides. Some adults remember talking to and playing with their guides, which would explain so-called imaginary friends. But when children learn to talk, and begin to describe what they see to adults, they usually get less than supportive messages. So in order to fit in and be accepted as 'normal,' most children shut down their ability to see guides.

Some say personal guides may be deceased loved ones, but others argue that departed relatives would be too close to serve as an impartial guide. Whoever your guides are, you can ask them to make

> *"And He will command his angels concerning you, to guard you carefully; they will lift you up in their hand so that you will not strike your foot against a stone."*
>
> *Luke 4:10-11*

> *A child's prayer:*
>
> *"There are four corners on my bed,*
>
> *There are four angels at my head-*
>
> *Matthew, Mark, Luke and John,*
>
> *Bless the bed I sleep on."*

themselves known. They may put a thought in your head, show up in your dreams or repeatedly put a nature or animal sign on your path to represent them. When I ask my guides to show me they are near, ladybugs appear, even in the dead of winter!

Past Lives/Reincarnation

Spice up your next dinner party with this subject: reincarnation. If you dare elicit opinions, your guests will probably fall into one of these three categories.

1. Those who believe in past lives

2. Those who do not believe and consider the past lives sacrilegious and blasphemous.

3. Those who are uncertain, curious and want more information.

Who Believes In Reincarnation?

According to the latest Gallup poll, the percentage of Americans who believe in reincarnation has grown from 21% to 25% over the last decade. A 1991 Gallup Poll said one-third of church going Christian teenagers believed in past lives. If you are curious about what other people believe, take your own poll.

My mission is not to make believers out of everyone, but to present the basic concepts and let people decide for themselves. *The Complete Idiot's Guide to Reincarnation* says, "Reincarnation is a concept, doctrine, or philosophy that states after death the soul is reborn in another form, in another body. For the soul, each body is a vehicle for learning. Furthermore, the thoughts, actions, and events of each lifetime influence future lifetimes." Many believe the spirit requires numerous material bodies to attain its perfection.

Those who believe in past lives say it helps them

"Men and women are not human beings having a spiritual experience, but rather, spiritual beings having a human experience."

Unknown

understand:

> *"Until we accept the fact that life itself is founded in mystery we shall learn nothing."*
>
> Henry Miller

- ❧ Why some people are more spiritually evolved than others. They've simply been around more times.
- ❧ Where many of their talents come from.
- ❧ Why certain behaviors are so difficult to change (soul carryover from other lifetimes).
- ❧ Love – or hatred – at first sight.
- ❧ Why people have fears/phobias for no apparent reason.
- ❧ Child prodigies and idiot savants.
- ❧ Traveling to different countries for the first time, yet feeling like they've been there before.
- ❧ The phenomena of déjà vu.

The list of believers in reincarnation is extensive: Hindus, Buddhists, Greeks, ancient Egyptians, Celts, Britons, Inuits, American Indians, Incas and Mayan civilizations, Gallics, Platonists and Pythagoreans all believed in past lives. Christianity is one of the only great world religions without a belief in reincarnation.

Why Not?

There are numerous theories on why reincarnation isn't supported in Christianity. Some scholars believe that reincarnation was taken for granted during the days of Jesus, so no one even thought to spell it out in the New Testament. Other scholars say that when the Bible was being written, there was indeed mention about reincarnation, but religious leaders at the time made a political decision to edit it out. The leaders perhaps feared they and the church would have less power if people knew they would have more than one life.

Dead Sea Scrolls

Biblical scholars cite the compelling information in the Dead Sea Scrolls, discovered by a shepherd near Israel and Jordan in 1947. It is widely believed that the Essenes, Christian Gnostics who lived during and after the time of Jesus, wrote the Dead Sea Scrolls. According to these transcribed scrolls, Jesus spoke frequently and easily about reincarnation and Karma, a version of the Golden Rule: what you do to others will come back to you.

Why Would Souls Want To Keep Coming Back?

For three reasons, according to author Rudolph Steiner: to advance as a soul, to pay off a debt (karma) and to help humanity.

What Is Past Life Regression Therapy?

Past life regression therapy is used by some therapists (not all are trained) to help their clients gain insights, understanding and uncover blocks. A client would first talk to their therapist about the problems they are experiencing. If past life regression therapy is recommended and desired, the client would be made comfortable (which may involve lying down) and put into a hypnotic state. This hypnotic state allows a client to access different parts of their mind, various dimensions of reality and additional sources of wisdom. The client is still aware of their current surroundings during this therapy session. It feels similar to watching a film in a movie theatre, but even more realistic and emotional. The amount of detail differs with each person, but many see specifics such as the type of shoes they were wearing, their hair color and physical surroundings.

Past life regression therapy is one of many

spiritual techniques that is available to assist you on your career and life journey. Learning about your past lives might help you understand your present life, obstacles, relationship struggles and themes. You may become more patient with yourself and more compassionate with others as a result of past life regression therapy.

Although some people can put themselves in an altered state of consciousness on their own, I highly recommend working with a trained, qualified professional who can provide guidance during the session and support afterward, so you can process your experience.

Ask around for a referral; you'd be surprised who has done this type of therapy. Or contact the Association for Past Life Research and Therapies for names of qualified therapists in your area.

RECOMMENDED READING

- *A Book of Angels*   by Sophy Burnham
- *Reflections of Heaven*   by Peter Shockey
- *Past Lives, Future Healing*   by Sylvia Browne
- *Past Lives, Past Selves, Many Lives, Many Masters*   by Brian Weiss, M.D.
- *Through Time Into Healing*
  by Brian Weiss, M.D.

CHAPTER 15

Faith, Grace, Solitude and Prayer

Faith

- Assurance
- Belief
- Certitude
- Confidence
- Reliance
- Sureness
- Trust

"Faith is daring the soul to go beyond what the eyes can see."

Anonymous

Everyone operates by some basic faith, or way of making sense of life. Faith is our beliefs about how the world works, how we were created and what the Divine Creator is all about. Faith is much more personal than religion.

Wilfred Cantwell Smith, a religion writer says "Faith is an orientation of the personality, to oneself, to one's neighbor, to the universe; a total response; a way of seeing whatever one sees and of handling whatever one handles; a capacity to live at more than a mundane level; to feel, to act in terms of a transcendent dimension."

The Hindu term for faith is Sridhar, which means, "to set one's heart on." James Fowler, author of *Stages of Faith* called faith "an alignment of the heart or will." Faith, it seems, is a universal feature of human

> *"Leap and the net will appear."*
>
> *Julia Cameron*

living. Acts of faith are similar in other countries, despite the variety of religious practices and beliefs.

Lack of faith

People like Mother Teresa seem to have been born with a larger dose of faith than most of us. Or perhaps she learned early on if she surrendered to God's will and help, things always had a way of working out.

The process of developing and deepening our faith is a continuous, lifelong journey for us all. If you want to work on deepening your faith, first, acknowledge to yourself and to the Creator that it's a growth area. Next, seek God's help by praying for grace. Turn small problems over to God and eventually work up to the big things. As you begin to see how much better things work out, you simultaneously build faith. Guidance and support may also be found in the company of a good spiritual counselor, pastor, priest or Rabbi. Contact your place of worship or ask around for a good referral.

Grace

I read somewhere that grace is God's love and protection, given free of charge to people who don't deserve it. Sara Ban Breathnach, in her book *Simple Abundance* describes grace as, "direct, divine intervention on our behalf that circumvents the laws of nature, time, space, cause and effect for our Highest Good."

Philip Yancey, author of *What's so Amazing About Grace* writes, "Grace is the Force, a spiritual energy field that protects and assists." Grace doesn't mean we are exempt from all difficult situations. It simply allows us to move through life in a state of love and protection as we deal with life's ups and downs.

I recently witnessed a perfect example of grace. My handyman husband was working in our solarium and was attempting to drain water wedged between two windowpanes. He purchased a special drill bit that "theoretically" was supposed to allow him to drill a clean hole through glass. Arms over his head, looking up, he started drilling. Suddenly there was a horrible cracking noise and the pane shattered into a million pieces directly above him! My husband was granted a few seconds to escape, which he did, before the pieces of glass came crashing down. That was grace in action.

> *"Courage is fear that has said its prayers."*
>
> Dorothy Bernard

How do you get grace? Simple. Ask God for it, accept and acknowledge it. It's that easy.

Think about times in your life when you were protected or even saved by God's protective grace. Then remember, when the world feels like it's crashing down around you, pray for grace. If you'd like to be blanketed in God's protective bubble, pray for grace. If you want Divine intervention to smooth out the rough edges and relationships in life, pray for grace. Expect it, watch for it, acknowledge it, and say a prayer of thanks to God, the giver of grace.

Prayer

"Explore daily the will of God." - Carl Jung

> *"Grace Happens"*
>
> Bumper Sticker

If the Creator already knows our every need, why should we pray? Prayer is more for us than for God. It's a way to establish, or reconnect with the Divine. We pray to know the Creator more fully and to experience a communion with the Divine. We pray for truth, awareness and for guidance.

Who To Pray To?

Although I am a Christian, I recognize there are many figures or deities that people worship. Who is it that you believe oversees the universe? A Higher Power of some kind? Is your Creator a male, father figure? Or perhaps you feel more comfortable petitioning Mother Earth? Many find comfort praying to Mary, the Mother of Jesus while others feel best praying directly to Jesus. Got a favorite patron saint? Go for it. Some feel a close connection to the Holy Spirit. By all means, pray to whoever feels closest and most approachable to you.

Time Of Day

There is no wrong time of day to pray. Many find that sunrise suits them best, whereas others prefer bedtime. Some kneel, lie down or sit when they pray, while others pray in motion, while commuting to work, walking a labyrinth, bike riding or hiking in solitude through the woods.

Pray daily, passionately and imaginatively. Pray powerfully and unedited. Talk to the Creator and tell Him or Her how you are doing and what you seek. Then listen for answers.

Consider Praying For:

- Fortitude
- Wisdom
- Strength
- Protection
- Guidance and visions
- Release of pain
- Healing for mind, body, spirit
- Patience
- Ability to know, feel and express love

> *"Just talk to God and make your life a living prayer."*
>
> Sylvia Browne

- Discernment to pursue the right things
- Energy

Thy Will Be Done

Larry Dossey is a medical doctor and leading expert on spirituality and medicine. In his book *Watch What You Pray For...You Just Might Get It,* he cautions against giving orders to God, or praying for specific outcomes. "The issue is not that we pray, but how we pray. When things go wrong, we invoke prayers with a highly specific outcome... Giving orders with prayer invites disaster," says Dossey. He goes on to say, "It's rather like hitting a card table from below, hoping that the pieces of the jigsaw puzzle on top will fall into greater order than before." Our well-intentioned prayers, if answered, might actually make matters worse because we don't understand and can't see the complexity and interconnectedness of life. Dossey tells us not to despair, to keep praying but to rely on the prayer expert - God! Our best prayer might come when we set aside our limited vision and personal agenda and pray "THY will be done" instead of "MY will be done."

Meditation

Meditation has been used for centuries as a form of prayer. Most recently, meditation has been embraced as a way to reduce stress and increase performance. The goal in meditation is to achieve an altered, peaceful state by clearing the mind of all distractions with the aid of focused breathing and sometimes visualization. Meditation can be done alone, with the aid of a tape.

"Life is God's novel. Let Him write it."

Isaac Bashevis Singer

Sample Meditation:

- Sit comfortably with your eyes closed. Keep

your back relatively straight. You may or may not want to cross your legs. Just don't lie down, as you'll likely fall asleep.

- Let your attention drift to your breathing.

- When thoughts and emotions or physical sensations arise, acknowledge and accept them, and allow them to pass through without judgment.

- Keep returning to focus on your breathing. Allow your mind to be free and clear of all thoughts.

- Meditation will most likely be difficult at first. It's hard to keep the mind still. Gradually increase the period you meditate by five or ten minutes. Meditation can be done outside with Mother Nature or inside to gentle, instrumental music.

Other Types Of Prayer

1. Informal conversation with God

2. Petition: asking for something specific

3. Formal: standard prayers said at church, synagogue or mosque

4. Movement: sacred dance, walking a labyrinth

5. Affirmation: prayer of thanksgiving

6. Grace: blessing before or after meals

Solitude

"There are voices which we hear in solitude, but they grow faint and inaudible as we enter the world."

Ralph Waldo Emerson

Eileen Caddy shares her words of wisdom about solitude. "All you need is deep within you waiting to unfold and reveal itself. All you have to do is be still and take time to seek what is within you, and you will surely find it." I instruct my clients to take at *least* 10-15 minutes a day of silence and solitude: more if they can squeeze it in.

Why Silence?

For starters, silence is great for self-care. Most of us are bombarded with auditory stimuli all day long: TVs, radio, stereo, voices, car horns, computer keyboard, telephones, cell-phones, pagers... the list of noisemakers is endless. Back when I worked in a corporate office we had "white noise," an office feature that was supposed to enhance our work environment by covering up our voices with a continuous, crackling noise. In practice, it irritated the heck out of people. Every night when the white noise would turn off, people's shoulders would drop and everyone would release a collective sigh of relief. What is the "white noise" in your life that's irritating the heck out of you? Can you turn it off or find a way to reduce your exposure to it?

"A mind too active is no mind at all."

Theodore Roethke

You'll also need silence for the second half of prayer, which works best as a two-way communication. Pray for direction and then listen in silence to hear God's response. However many minutes you spend praying, just add one or two more minutes listening.

Necessary For Thinking

If you've ever exclaimed, "It's so noisy I can't hear myself think" then you know silence is essential for thought. Since you'll be doing a great deal of thinking, reflecting, and contemplating, you'll need healthy doses of daily silence. Use these strategies to get more quiet time in your busy, noisy life.

- Get up early, before everyone else in the house is up.
- Stay up late, after everyone goes to bed.
- Walk the dog.

- Go for a walk in the woods.
- Shovel snow.
- Do gardening or yard work by yourself.
- Take up running
- Turn off your radio in the car.
- Unplug the TV for a month.
- Go away on a silent retreat
- Ask a friend with a cabin if you can stay there, by yourself.
- Housesit, or pet sit for friends or relatives on vacation.

> *"For me, a long five or six mile walk helps. And one must go alone and everyday."*
>
> *Brenda Ueland*

RECOMMENDED READING

- *The Power of Prayer Around the World* by Glenn Mosley and Joanna Hill

PART 6

Manifest Your Dreams

MOVE ON WITH GOALS AND ACTION PLANS

CHAPTER 16

Goal Setting, Problem Solving and Action Plans

Think of people you know who are movers and shakers, always accomplishing and achieving great things. They have learned to identify precisely what they want, and know how to chart a course to get there. That's goal setting.

"Goals are dreams with deadlines."

Unknown

Benefits Of Goal Setting

The benefits of goal setting are vast and varied. Goal setting keeps you focused, helping you discern what is important in life as opposed to things that are mere distractions. Setting and accomplishing goals makes life richer and can boost your self-esteem, motivation and performance. By setting goals, you are setting yourself up for success through learning, growing, changing and accomplishing all that's important to you.

Hint: Although the focus of this book is on careers and professional life, this format works well with personal goals including family, financial, physical health, spirituality, leisure, community service, etc.

Where To Start

Start by clearing your calendar. Grab three or four consecutive, uninterrupted hours to work. Get a pad of paper and pen. Keep it simple by starting with these four contemplation questions. Write down the answer when you can.

1. What do I want?

2. Why do I want it?

3. When do I want it by?

4. What am I willing to do to achieve it?

> "Whatever God's dream about man may be, it seems certain it cannot come true unless man cooperates."
>
> *Stella Terrill Mann*

After you spend a fair amount of time contemplating and answering these four questions, you can move on to setting goals, but reader beware: there are a few mistakes to avoid. When people set goals that are too vague, they never know if they've accomplished their goal. Be sure to make your goal specific. Another mistake is to set a goal that is either too difficult, or too easy. Avoid setting too many goals at a time. Be sure the goal is actually something you want and give yourself adequate time to achieve it in a systematic approach.

Useful goals have these seven major elements. When writing down your goals, make sure they are:

1. Specific

2. Measurable

3. Challenging

4. Realistic

5. Attached to a completion date or deadline

6. Truly yours, not someone else's

7. Written down and kept visible

If you fail to achieve your goal, ask yourself if it was because you were lacking information, education or using an incorrect technique. You don't want to give up early on a goal, but there can be wisdom in revisions.

Once you have set a goal, the next step is to list specific intermediate and daily tasks based on your long-range goal. For example, Sam's long-range goal is to start his own catering business. He has identified three intermediate steps to get things moving.

> *"Things do not change. We change."*
>
> *Henry David Thoreau*

Sam's Intermediate Steps

1. Interview 3-4 people who run a catering business

2. Take a class on how to write a business plan

3. Write a business plan and apply for a loan.

From this list, he will write down daily tasks on his calendar.

Sam's Daily Tasks

Monday – Call the local community colleges and request a business catalogue. Look them over when they arrive and sign up for the earliest class on how to write a business plan.

Tuesday – Get 5 names of catering companies from the yellow pages and call the businesses. Request an informational interview with the owners. Schedule interviews next week.

Wednesday – Call 3 local banks and ask what the interest rate is on a $50,000 secured business loan. Inquire about the process and request forms.

Problem Solving

Barbara Sher, author of *Wishcraft- How to Get What you Really Want,* is a career counselor with a can do, take charge attitude. She states, "There is no strategic problem that can't be solved." What a powerful, liberating philosophy to live by.

Make problem-solving manageable and productive by following these seven sequential steps.

7 Steps To Productive Problem Solving

<u>Steps</u>	<u>My True Life Examples</u>
1. Define problem	I can't write my book due to constant interruptions
2. List desired state	Hours of uninterrupted writing time to finish book.
3. Analyze causes	Kids, phones, clients, students, neighbors, dog, husband, sales calls, repair and delivery people.
4. Identify/ brainstorm solutions	a. Tell kids, "No interruptions unless you're bleeding."
	b. Apply for writer residency
	c. Stay weekends at convents
	d. Use a friend's cabin
	e. Rent a writing studio
5. Select the best solution(s)	Options b, c, d, e
6. Develop an action plan.	Fill out residency forms. Call my friend and ask to use her cabin.
	Schedule weekends away at convents.
	Rent writing studio.
7. Implement	Show up for two-week writing residency and write.
	Schedule dates at friend's

cabin. Show up and write!

Schedule one weekend away per month at convents.

Rent writing studio at Loft Literary Center.

It's also important to have an ongoing evaluation process to determine the effectiveness of your action plan. In my case, all options worked well and were relatively cheap.

Brainstorming

Brainstorming is a wonderful, creative technique for producing multiple solutions to any problem. You may have used this technique at work or in your personal life, but here are a few suggestions for the best brainstorming possible.

Be sure to define the problem at its basic level. Once you have clearly defined the problem, enter the brainstorming session, striving for quantity over quality. As you free-flowingly write down every solution that enters your mind, be careful not to judge, censor, criticize or evaluate any of your answers: the more unusual the solutions, the better.

Individual Versus Group Brainstorming

Individual brainstorming might produce a wide range of ideas, but there may be times when the diversity of a group brainstorm will be more effective. If you try brainstorming alone and get stuck, invite a half-dozen of your closest friends over for a light dinner and problem-solving session. Tell people in advance what the problem is so they can contemplate possible solutions. Remind everyone to bring their address book, so they can share professional contacts and resources.

Mind Maps

One student described mind-maps as "a brain dump on paper." Mind maps are a great way to organize, summarize, evaluate and consolidate vast amounts of information onto one page. In my opinion, mind-maps are easier to create, review and recall than conventional outlines. It's perfect for creative souls who are loosely organized and non-linear thinkers.

Supplies Needed

1. Preferably a large sheet of paper, but any size will work

2. Various colored markers or pens

How To Draw a Mind Map

1. Draw a circle in the middle of the page.

2. Write the subject in the middle of the circle.

3. As you think of your main categories, draw lines out from the circle. Label each categories with brief headings.

4. Sub-headings can be inserted under or spun off from the main categories with a line. Label with simple phrases.

5. Mind-maps can be used to order things sequentially. After constructing the main categories and sub-headings, go back and number accordingly.

Tips For Constructing Magnificent Mind-Maps

1. Limit words to single words or simple, short phrases.

2. Draw pictures, or symbols to convey information. Visuals and pictures help with recall.

3. Color can be used to visually separate ideas.

4. Use arrows to indicate cause and effect.

5. Let branches indicate connections.

6. Leave space to add additional details later.

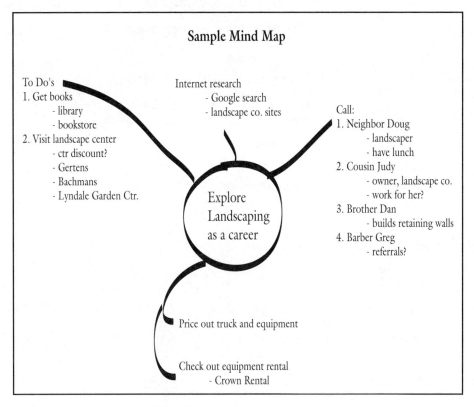

Sample Mind Map

To Do's
1. Get books
   - library
   - bookstore
2. Visit landscape center
   - ctr discount?
   - Gertens
   - Bachmans
   - Lyndale Garden Ctr.

Internet research
   - Google search
   - landscape co. sites

Call:
1. Neighbor Doug
   - landscaper
   - have lunch
2. Cousin Judy
   - owner, landscape co.
   - work for her?
3. Brother Dan
   - builds retaining walls
4. Barber Greg
   - referrals?

Explore Landscaping as a career

Price out truck and equipment

Check out equipment rental
   - Crown Rental

Your Turn

Think of a problem related to your career quest. Grab some paper and follow the seven steps for productive problem solving. At step four, use the brainstorming technique to create possible solutions. At step six, draw a mind map depicting your action plan.

1. Define problem

2. List desired state

3. *Analyze causes*

4. *Identify possible solutions (brainstorm)*

5. *Select the best solution(s)*

6. *Develop an action plan (draw a mind map)*

7. *Implement and evaluate progress*

RECOMMENDED READING

- *Wishcraft- How to Get What You Really Want* by Barbara Sher
- *Live the Life you Love in Ten Easy Step-by-Step Lessons*   by Barbara Sher
- *Making Your Dreams Come True* by Marcia Weider

CHAPTER 17

Affirmations and Creative Transitions

Affirmations

Scott Adams, creator of the famous Dilbert cartoon, transformed his life with hard work and this simple affirmation: "I am the next, world famous cartoonist." He recited this daily for a number of years until he became 'the next, world famous cartoonist.'

"Creation is only the projection into form of that which already exists."

Shrimad Bhagavatam

Affirmations are a powerful technique used to condition the mind into a healthier, positive state. Simply put, an affirmation is positive self-talk, or a prescription for an area of your life you want to improve.

Working With Affirmations

Write your affirmation in the current tense and always write first person.

"I am blessed with abundance" works better than "Some day I will be wealthy."

Be sure to write your affirmations down, focusing on just one or two relevant intentions at a time. Even if you have your affirmation memorized, keep it visible: bathroom mirror, in the car, on your desk, or wherever you spend a great deal of time. Keeping your affirmation visible will remind you to recite it. Say it out loud, several times a day and try reciting your

> *"If you can imagine it, you can achieve it. If you can dream it, you can become it."*
>
> *William Arthur Ward*

affirmation in the mirror for a more powerful effect. You can use affirmations in a number of ways:

Change Behaviors

Terre Thomas, a mother, writer and successful business owner who worked from home needed to do a better job focusing. Her affirmation was: "I am a master at keeping out annoying distractions.

Deal With Fear

I used this affirmation to counteract my fear when I became self-employed. "The world is abundant and meets all my needs."

Improve Attitude

"I move beyond old limitations and allow myself the freedom to succeed."

Enhance Spirituality and Boost Confidence in Decision Making

"I accept Divine Guidance into my life and make great choices with ease."

Feel Better

"I am secure, loved, protected and supported by the Divine, all my angels and my earthly companions."

There is no limit to what you can use affirmations for. Use the space below to write an affirmation of your own.

> *"Desire, ask, believe, receive."*
>
> *Stella Terrill Mann*

_____

_____

_____

_____

_____

Creative Transitions

Clients who despise their jobs frequently ask me, "How will I know when it's my time to leave?" While there are no pat answers, there are telltale signs.

"We must be willing to get rid of the life we've planned, so as to have the life that is waiting for us."

Joseph Campbell

It's Close To Quitting Time If:

1. Sunday evenings depress you.

2. The quality of your work has suffered, but you don't care.

3. You arrive consistently late for work.

4. You call in sick when healthy.

5. You've become emotionally distant from co-workers.

6. Your job has taken a toll on your mental and physical health to the point family and friends have begun to express their concerns.

7. Upon hearing rumors of company layoffs, you pray, "Please Lord. Let it be me!"

8. You don't have enough work to keep busy, but lack motivation or desire to seek new assignments.

9. The lights around your desk or workspace burn out frequently.

10. Time drags and you constantly watch the clock.

There was a song back in the 70's that described fifty ways to leave your lover. Here are 25 ways to leave your job. Some are silly, others quite serious, and a couple may be a stretch. You decide which is which.

1. Go on an extended vacation and forget to come back to work.

2. Take a sabbatical

3. Transfer.

4. Simply quit. Either give a two week notice or storm out dramatically: your choice.

5. Medical/ family leave can provide time to contemplate other careers. (Warning: Don't have a baby just to avoid career decisions!)

6. Get fired.

7. Ask to be "let go" with a decent severance package.

8. Quit and do temp work awhile: wait tables, drive a school bus, work in retail.

9. Win the lottery

10. Encourage a rich relative to include you in their will.

11. Start your own business

12. Marry money (caution: if you don't love the person, you'll earn every penny)

13. Retire early, then start another career.

14. Go part-time: gradually reduce your hours until you no longer work there.

15. Move.

16. Apply for an artist grant. Become an artist in residency for a year.

17. Line up sponsors. Bike, walk or sail around the world, then write a best-selling book about it.

18. Let Hollywood discover you.

19. See if your partner/spouse can earn more money.

20. Move back in with your parents, grandma,

sister, brother, uncle, aunt.

21. Be a live-in nanny till you figure out what's next.

22. Buy a cheap log cabin and live off the land.

23. Join a religious order.

24. Volunteer for the Peace Corp.

25. Sell everything and become a professional house sitter/pet sitter.

Add five ideas of your own.

1. _____

   _____

2. _____

   _____

4. _____

   _____

4. _____

   _____

5. _____

   _____

> *"The world's round and the place which may seem like the end, may also be only the beginning."*
>
> *Ivy Baker Priest*

Six True Life Transitions

1. Greg, an executive in the utility business asked to be let go from his job of 20 years. He requested and received a six-month severance package, complete with benefits.

2. Jim was downsized from his job as a manufacturing engineer. Since he suffered from chronic fatigue syndrome, instead of searching for another job, he chose to reduce his living

expenses, tap his savings, then study and trade in the stock market.

3. Shirley, a licensed psychologist grew tired with the ups and downs of working for a health insurance organization, so she started her own private practice. Most of her clients followed her.

4. Barbara was a burnt out mom and research librarian from the Midwest who felt the need for a change. She got on the Internet and located a one-semester faculty position at a community college in Sacramento, California. This "working sabbatical" provided a much-needed respite from her job, parenting responsibilities and a bitter winter.

5. Diana, a Ph.D. health educator, relied on temp work to pay the bills when she was between jobs on two separate occasions: once when her position was unexpectedly eliminated and another time when she quit an emotionally toxic job.

6. My personal favorite: I left my corporate job by speaking up and acting out. " My boss finally pulled me aside and said, "I can't manage you anymore. I think it's your time to leave." Thankfully, I had been moonlighting as a freelance writer for a year and had already started my own company. I agreed; it was my time to leave.

> *"Ask, and it shall be given to you; seek and ye shall find; knock and it shall be opened unto you."*
>
> *Matthew 7:7*

Have hope. All is in divine order. Trust the Creator to orchestrate your divine exit when the time is right. You can help manifest your transition by applying the four P's: Prayer, persistence, problem-solving and patience.

With time, you can – and will – find a way out!

Where Do I Go From Here?

In the Bible, the book of Ecclesiastics teaches us there is a time for everything. It is the right time for your career quest. Move forward by heeding these suggestions:

> *"Expect your every need to be met, expect the answer to every problem, expect abundance on every level, expect to grow spiritually."*
>
> *Eileen Caddy*

- Claim this month and year as the official kick off to your career quest.

- Ask for support from spouse, friends, partners, and children. Be specific!

- If currently employed, release yourself emotionally and spiritually from your job.

- Keep a running list of activities that energize you.

- Try one new experience each week to uncover hidden, untapped talents.

- Practice good self-care habits.

- Live simply; pay off debts, build your savings.

- Remain open to the process. Take breaks when you need it.

- Pray for guidance. Then listen, watch for, receive and integrate it.

- Volunteer.

- Increase reading, decrease TV watching.

- Buy a dream journal. Reflect, interpret and apply the wisdom.

- Dedicate 10-15 minutes a day to solitude and silence.

- Trust yourself.

Career Quest Index

E

employment 18, 21

F

failure 94, 101, 108, 111
faith 7, 81, 108, 135, 137, 139, 141
fear 24, 83, 87, 93, 94, 95, 96, 97, 98, 99, 100, 101, 102, 109, 124, 137, 154
Feng
  Shui 59, 64
financial 7, 28, 65, 67, 69, 71, 73, 75, 77, 78, 79, 81, 82, 94
  resources 77
Fowler, James 135
friendships 87

G

Gardner, Howard 43
goal
  setting 7, 60, 145, 147, 149, 151, 153
grace 7, 135, 136, 137, 139, 140, 141
gratitude 71, 72

H

Hardy, Robert 102
health 25, 27, 74, 75, 88
  issues 23, 25, 26, 27, 28, 29, 30, 71, 84, 88, 100, 102, 103, 104, 111, 118, 121, 145,
    155, 158
higher
  purpose 23, 31, 32, 33, 35, 36, 37, 79
  self 7, 23, 25, 31, 32, 33, 35, 37, 53, 112, 116, 138
humor 99
Hyden, Ruth 65
Hyder, Tom 23

I

inspiration 37, 118, 122, 127
intuition 7, 115, 116, 117, 119

J

Johnson, Dave 50

K

Keech, Patsy 99

W

wake
  up
    calls 24, 25, 26, 28, 29, 30, 123
Williams, Marianne 42

X

Y

Yancey, Philip 136

Z

About the Author

Mary Rose Remington is a career counselor who has helped thousands of people climb out of their career rut and find work they love. In addition to providing client consultations, she writes two syndicated coumns, is a frequent guest on television and radio shows nationwide, and travels the country conducting motivational seminars.

Photo: Hilary N. Bullok Photography, Inc.

Speaker

Need a speaker for your next gathering? Mary Rose is a passionate, energetic and experienced presenter. Her message about finding purposeful, passionate work resonates with audiences and is a perfect fit for business and professional conferences, women's and men's organizations and church groups of all denominations. She is a master at customizing her presentations to each audience. To schedule an appearance, or for more information please visit her website at www.maryremington.com and click on "Keynote Presentations."

Private Consultations

Mary Rose earned her Master's Degree in Counseling and Guidance in 1985 and has counseled clients on career issues for over twenty years. She combines her practical coaching skills, business expertise, intuitive abilities and a "can-do" attitude to help people find passionate careers and more meaningful lives. She is available for a limited number of consultations each month. To book an individual phone consultation with Mary Rose, visit her website and click on "Consultations."

Syndicated Columnist and Author

Since 1995, millions of loyal readers have enjoyed her internationally syndicated column, ***Common-day Spirituality***, where the wheels of Christian spirituality hit the road of daily life. View her current columns online at www.thecatholicspirit.com.

Her new column, ***Balancing Act***, provides practical advice on careers, kids, home life and healthy living. Readers can subscribe to this free monthly column at www.maryremington.com. Simply click on "Columns".

Career Quest - A Practical And Spiritual Guide To Finding Your Life's Passion, is her first book. Mary Rose lives with her husband and three children in a suburb of St. Paul, Minnesota.